HIDDEN
— *in* —
HISTORY

The Untold Stories of Female

Artists, Musicians, and Writers

By Myra Faye Turner

HIDDEN IN HISTORY: THE UNTOLD STORIES OF FEMALE ARTISTS, MUSICIANS, AND WRITERS

Copyright © 2018 Atlantic Publishing Group, Inc.

1405 SW 6th Avenue • Ocala, Florida 34471 • Phone 352-622-1825 • Fax 352-622-1875
Website: www.atlantic-pub.com • Email: sales@atlantic-pub.com
SAN Number: 268-1250

Library of Congress Cataloging-in-Publication Data

Names: Turner, Myra Faye, author.
Title: Hidden in history : the untold stories of female artists, musicians, and writers / by Myra Faye Turner.
Description: Ocala, Florida : Atlantic Publishing Group, Inc., [2018] | Series: Hidden in history | Includes bibliographical references and index. | Audience: Ages 12-18. | Audience: Grades 7 to 8.
Identifiers: LCCN 2018018002 (print) | LCCN 2018032773 (ebook) | ISBN 9781620235645 (ebook) | ISBN 9781620235638 (pbk. : alk. paper) | ISBN 9781620235652 (library edition : alk. paper) | ISBN 1620235633
Subjects: LCSH: Women artists—United States—Biography—Juvenile literature.
Classification: LCC NX511.5 (ebook) | LCC NX511.5 .T87 2018 (print) | DDC 700.92/52 [B]—dc23
LC record available at https://lccn.loc.gov/2018018002

Printed in the United States

PROJECT MANAGER: Danielle Lieneman
COVER DESIGN AND INTERIOR LAYOUT: Nicole Sturk

Over the years, we have adopted a number of dogs from rescues and shelters. First there was Bear and after he passed, Ginger and Scout. Now, we have Kira, another rescue. They have brought immense joy and love not just into our lives, but into the lives of all who met them.

We want you to know a portion of the profits of this book will be donated in Bear, Ginger and Scout's memory to local animal shelters, parks, conservation organizations, and other individuals and nonprofit organizations in need of assistance.

– Douglas & Sherri Brown,
President & Vice-President of Atlantic Publishing

Table of Contents

Part I: Wordsmiths

Chapter One

Part II: Visual Artists

Part III: Performing Artists

Zora Neale Hurston, Mayo Angelou, Frida Kahlo, Georgia O'Keeffe, Isadora Duncan, Martha Graham, Diana Ross, Adele, Marilyn Monroe, and Jennifer Lawrence — what do these women have in common? You're probably familiar with most (if not all) of the names on this list. These queens are examples of women who reached prominence in their artistic endeavors.

Here's another question for you. Varina Davis, Amelia Bloomer, Edmonia Lewis, Romaine Brooks, Carmen Amaya, Hattie McDaniel, the International Sweethearts of Rhythm, Maria Tallchief, Anna May Wong, and Lakshmi Shankar — what do these women have in common? I'm guessing you're probably not familiar with most (or any) of these women.

Like the names in the previous paragraph, these queens were also leaders in their artistic fields. The difference is that most never received the props they deserved. Their names aren't written in most school history books, but they are exceptional women. These brave women kicked open doors so that other women could walk through.

This book will shine a spotlight on exceptional female artists, writers, and musicians — women who have previously been hidden from history. By the end of this book, you will know their names *and* their stories. And like the Olympic torch, please pass their stories on.

(Left) Maya Angelou poses for a portrait in 2009, when she was 81 years old.
(Right) Hattie McDaniel poses for a portrait in 1939, when she was 44 years old.

Women in the arts

Historically there have always been gifted women artists. Unfortunately, these same women haven't received as much praise as their male counterparts. In some disciplines, women artists have faced barriers to entry. For example, visual artists often "... have faced challenges due to gender biases, from finding difficulty in training to selling their work and gaining recognition," wrote Camille Gajewski in her essay, "A Brief History of Women in Art." [1]

To get a foot in the door, some female writers used male pen names. The Victorian era novelist George Eliot, for example, was the pen name of Mary Ann Evans. J. K. Rowling (aka Joanne Rowling) intentionally used initials

1. Gajewski, 2015.

for her Harry Potter series. Her publisher didn't think the target audience (middle-grade boys) would read a book about wizards written by a woman. Because she didn't have a middle name, Rowling chose "K" for Kathleen, her grandmother's name.

Choosing to live an artistic life isn't always easy for artist of any gender. Women often face additional challenges as they struggle to balance duties as wives and mothers, while working full- or part-time.

Although chasing your artistic dreams can be difficult, there's help for artists. The federal government, non-profit organizations, and private donors often provide grants, endowments, and financial backing to artists. Artists also sometimes receive financial support from family, friends, or benefactors.

(Left) Author J. K. Rowling is photographed here at a reading of *Harry Potter and the Sorcerer's Stone* for an Easter event at the White House. (Right) Marry Ann Evans, aka George Eliot, poses for a portrait by Sir Frederic William Burton in 1865.

The Works Project Administration

One past federally funded job-creating program for artists was the Works Project Administration (WPA). President Franklin D. Roosevelt created the WPA in 1935. The WPA provided jobs for millions of citizens during the Great Depression.

The Great Depression (1929-1939) was a period of economic decline in the United States. This depressed period included the stock market crash, failed banks, and severe unemployment. The WPA included many programs for artists, under the *Federal One* umbrella. The *Federal One* program included five projects:

- *The Federal Art Project* supported projects for visual artists including sculptors, graphic artists, and photographers. The program provided jobs for over 5,000 visual artists.

- *The Federal Music Project* provided work for musicians who performed for 3 million people each week. Over 16,000 musicians found work because of this program.

- *The Federal Theatre Project* welcomed audiences for live performances and beamed radio broadcast to entertain citizens at home. At one point, 13,000 people were employed thanks to this program.

- *The Federal Writers Project* employed 7,000 writers to create the American Guide Series. These guides covered 48 states and several regions. They covered local and cultural history. The writers in this program also produced other works including slave narratives and folklore collections. Many writers were employed as researchers or provided writing and editorial services.

- **The Historical Records Survey** employed archivists to preserve historical data. It was the smallest of the programs, but this important project is the reason we have much of the historical records we have today.

All WPA programs ended in 1943. Thankfully, programs such as those administered by the National Endowment for the Arts (NEA) and state arts agencies, continue to support artists today.

Eleanor Roosevelt was an active force alongside her husband, FDR. She is pictured here at a WPA site in Des Moines, Iowa.

How this book is organized

This book is organized into three sections: **wordsmiths, visual artists,** and **performing artists.** Each chapter profiles one female artist (Chapter 9 highlights a musical group). You'll learn basic background information about each artist before moving on to discuss her accomplishments in her field. We'll end the chapter by discussing her legacy and impact on future generations of artists who have also chosen the same path.

Part I
Wordsmiths

Merriam-Webster defines "wordsmith" as:

> *"A person who works with words; especially a skillful writer."*[2]

There are many types of writers. Here's a short list:

- Journalist/newspaper reporters

- Essayists

- Playwrights

- Screenwriters

- Bloggers

- Novelists

- Columnists

- Poets

---

2. Merriam-Webster, 2017.

- Short story writers

- Copywriters

- Technical writers

Each wordsmith normally focuses on one type of writing. It's not unusual for writers, however, to dabble in more than one literary form. A writer can also work as a full-time staff writer or freelance for different publishers. The writer for this informative guide is a full-time freelance writer. I normally write at my desk in my home office, previously known as my son's bedroom (don't worry, I moved him to a bigger bedroom). Today as I edit the first section of this book, I'm working from my bed because it's dark and rainy outside. My bed is so much cozier. But I digress. The point I'm making is that writers often write from home, the beach, the local coffee shop, or the library. We have today's technological advances to thank for this privilege.

Writers may use their legal name or a "nom de plume," a pen name or pseudonym. A writer may work alone or collaborate with a writer partner. If you're considering a career as a writer, the possibilities are endless.

Part I of this book highlights two great, but lesser known, wordsmiths: Varina Anne "Winnie" Davis and Amelia Bloomer. In addition to being great writers, these two women had other claims to fame, which we'll discuss in their respective chapters. So let's get started.

Chapter One

Varina Anne "Winnie" Davis

Daughter of the Confederacy

Daughter of the Confederacy

Young Varina Anne "Winnie" Davis often accompanied her father when he traveled. Winnie's father was Jefferson Davis, former president of the Confederate States of America. During the Civil War, 11 southern states decided they wanted to secede, or leave the Union. These states opposed the abolition of slavery. They decided to form their own government. They called their new regime the Confederate States of America. On February 18, 1861, these states elected Jefferson Davis as president of their new nation.

Jefferson Davis was said to have resembled his presidential contemporary, Abraham Lincoln.

When the war ended in 1865, the Confederate States became part of the Union again. Although they lost the war, Davis was a revered and popular figure for many southerners. Davis traveled often to participate in veteran events.

During one of her father's trips Winnie was anointed with the title, "Daughter of the Confederacy"— a name that clung to her like a drowsy cat for the rest of her life.

On April 30, 1886, Winnie was accompanying her father on a trip to West Point, Georgia. Davis was traveling to unveil a series of Confederate monuments. When they arrived at the event, Davis was too ill to speak. A large crowd gathered outside, awaiting the arrival of the former president. While the crowd lingered, a band played in the background.

Not wanting to disappoint the flock, Georgia Governor John B. Gordon (who was hosting the event) had an idea. He grabbed Winnie by the arm and propelled her to the platform. Gordon introduced Winnie as "... the daughter of the Confederacy ... the war baby of our old chieftain." [3]

Winnie was as surprised as the onlookers when she was thrust into the spotlight. Like an actress facing the camera for the first time, Winnie smiled, then waved shyly. The veterans roared their approval. Winnie didn't speak but the crowd was enamored with her. From that moment on, she bore the title like a crown in life — and in death.

The tour and Winnie's new title, "... marked the beginning of the Winnie's rise as the most powerful female symbol of the 'Lost Cause'," wrote Heath Hardage Lee in her book, *Winnie Davis: Daughter of the Lost Cause.* [4]

---

3. Lee, 2014.
4. Lee, 2014.

This side profile of Winnie Davis was commissioned in 1864.

The "Daughter of the Confederacy" also achieved literary success as an author and journalist. Before we get to that, let's start at her beginning.

FAST FACT "The Lost Cause" was the belief held by southern Confederates that although the South lost the Civil War, they put up a noble fight.

Historic birth

Varina Anne Davis was born June 27, 1864. She was the second daughter and last child of Varina Howell Davis and Jefferson Davis. She was nicknamed "Winnie" at birth, but didn't receive her formal name until a year later. We use her nickname throughout this chapter, to distinguish the younger Varina from her mother.

 Winnie is an American Indian name meaning "bright or sunny." [5]

The Davises had six children: four boys and two girls. Tragically, three of the sons died young:

- Samuel Emory Davis died of measles when he was two (1852).

- Joseph Evan Davis died in 1864 from injuries sustained when he fell from a balcony. He was five. Varina was pregnant with Winnie at the time.

- 11-year-old William Howell Davis died in 1872 of diphtheria.

The couple's last son, Jefferson Davis, Jr., died of yellow fever when he was 21 (1878). Daughter Margaret Howell Davis Hayes was 54 when she died in 1909.

Winnie was born one year before the end of the Civil War. She was born in Richmond, Virginia in a mansion nicknamed "The White House of the Confederacy." The family spent much of their time in the library. They called this space the "snuggery" because it was the warmest room in the mansion. Richmond residents called the estate the Brockenbrough Mansion (for the family the house was originally built for in 1818) or the Gray House (because of its color).

In addition to their own kids, the Davis' family reportedly cared for a young black child named James Limber. Limber was the orphaned son of a free black woman. Supposedly, Varina rescued the young boy when she saw him being mistreated on the streets. She brought him home with her, and he became a playmate to the Davis' kids.

---

5. Harding, 2010.

During most of the Civil War, Richmond was untouched. But on April 2, 1865, Davis was notified Union troops were advancing on the city. There was little hope of holding the troops off. Davis had no choice but flee.

Fearing his family might be captured and used as bait to get him to surrender, he sent Varina and his kids to Charlotte, North Carolina three days earlier. The entourage included Colonel Burton Harrison, Jefferson's private secretary; secretary of the treasury George Trenholm's two daughters; Varina's sister, Margaret; James Limber; two servants Ellen and James Jones; and James Morgan, their armed escort.

Escape from Richmond

On April 2, Union troops invaded Richmond. The town was looted and set ablaze. Residents scampered for their lives. Some Confederate soldiers burned businesses to stop the Union soldiers from getting their paws on anything of value.

The mansion survived. President Lincoln even paid a visit to Richmond. Along with his son Tad, the president visited the ruined Confederate capital on April 4. While in Richmond, Lincoln toured the home of the man who had been a thorn in his side for four years.

On April 9, Confederate General Robert E. Lee surrendered to Union General Ulysses S. Grant. Meanwhile, Varina and her troop continued traveling toward South Carolina, not knowing what was happening to the family patriarch.

Rosy-cheeked Winnie was not quite a year old. The older kids were tired, dirty, and hungry as they traveled by train, on foot, and in wagons.

On April 14, tragedy rocked the nation. Actor John Wilkes Booth assassinated President Abraham Lincoln. The president was watching a performance at Ford's Theatre in Washington, D.C. at the time of his demise.

Booth said that by killing Lincoln he hoped to get the rest of the Confederate troops fired up and continue fighting. The Confederates didn't see it that way. They felt the Union would blame the Confederates for Lincoln's death.

They were right. On May 2, President Johnson placed a $100,000 bounty on Davis' head. Davis was now a fugitive as he fled Richmond trying to catch up with beloved family. On May 9, he caught up with them near Irwinville, Georgia. He planned to spend the night, then travel solo to Texas.

 The **$100,000** bounty in 1865 is the equivalent of about **$1,450,908.77** in 2018.

But escape would not come for the president of the Confederate States of America. Union soldiers captured Davis. He was marched off to Fort Monroe in Hampton Roads, Virginia.

The disgraced president was imprisoned for two years at Fort Monroe. It was within these prison walls that young Winnie and her father became close. The precocious toddler was the only one of Davis' kids allowed to visit the former president.

"She would put her arms round his neck, and he would clasp her to his bosom, forgetting everything for the moment except the baby fingers that were pressed against his cheeks and the blue eyes that looked into his. It would be hard to over estimate the comfort she afforded him while he was treading the winepress of bitterness and humiliation," wrote Chiles Clifton Ferrell in *The Daughter of the Confederacy* (1899).[6]

After his release, Davis reunited with his family in Montreal, Canada. Varina, her mother, sister, and the kids had found solace there.

The family moved to Lennoxville, a small town near Montreal, Canada in late 1867. They then traveled to Quebec, before settling in Liverpool, England in the summer of 1868. The Davis' returned to the United States in 1869, when Davis was offered a job as president of the Carolina Insurance Company. The family settled in Memphis, Tennessee.

The job wouldn't last long. The company was sold in 1873 and Davis resigned. He decided to look for work in England. When he returned in June 1874, Winnie was 10.

A southerner abroad

Winnie received much of her early schooling at the Memphis Female Seminary. The small school had five teachers. The girls were taught music, art, and languages. Winnie's parents also supplemented her formal training at home.

When Winnie was 13, her parents sent her to Misses Friedländers School in Karlsruhe, Germany.

Winnie thrived in the school, which had a rigorous curriculum and strict rules. The bright tween was soon at the top of her class.

---

6. Ferrell, 1899.

While Winnie was excelling abroad, there was scandal at home. In 1877, her father moved into a cottage owned by Sarah Dorsey, a wealthy widow and fervent supporter of the Confederacy. The cottage was on Dorsey's estate, Beauvoir, located in Gulfport, Mississippi. Davis was working on his memoirs. Dorsey was a writer and she helped Davis by reading his drafts, taking dictation, and doing research.

Sarah Dorsey

Sarah Anne Ellis Dorsey was an accomplished writer originally from Natchez, Mississippi. Her father, Thomas George Percy Ellis was a member of the prominent Percy family. The Percy's produced several successful writers.

Dorsey's first work was *Agnes Graham,* serialized in the literary magazine *Southern Literary Messenger* (1863-64). She followed this with a biography of Henry Watkins Allen, governor of Louisiana (published in 1866), *Lucia Dare* (1867), and *Panola* (1877).

Varina was living in England because of her "ill-health"(her ailment was never clearly identified). Dorsey was Varina's former classmate. There was juicy gossip that Davis and Dorsey were involved in a romantic affair. When the news reached Varina, she was outraged, but she didn't hurry home to see what her husband was up to.

Talks of Davis' infidelity had driven a wedge in the marriage. When Varina Davis finally returned from England, she lived with her married daughter, Margaret Hayes, in Memphis.

Dorsey revised her will in 1878. She left her estate to Davis. This added fuel to the gossip fire that something romantic was going on between the two. In the will, Winnie became Sarah's heir, also. If Jefferson Davis died before Winnie, she would inherit Beauvoir, not her mother.

After Varina finally arrived at Beauvoir in May 1878, she was furious. She'd had to deal with the quiet whispers of possible infidelity. Things cooled down somewhat when Dorsey agreed to sell Beauvoir to Davis. He made the first of three installments in February 1879. In June of that same year, Dorsey died of breast cancer. Davis insisted on paying the remaining two payments, even though he had inherited Dorsey's estate.

Meanwhile, young Winnie continued to do well in school. She had an interest in and excelled at drawing, writing, music, and painting.

Miss Varina Anne (WINNIE) Davis
The Daughter of the Confederacy

This illustration exemplifies Winnie Davis' title as Daughter of the Confederacy.

Young Varina returns

In 1882, Winnie returned to the United States. She was now a young woman of 18. She returned with knowledge of art, music, literature ... and a German accent. Before leaving Germany, she spent a few months in France, where she studied the language and traveled.

By all accounts, Winnie was her father's favorite child; not much had changed during her years abroad. Winnie and her father were inseparable.

The two spent a lot of time alone together. Davis even converted a room next to his study into an art studio for Winnie.

As we read at the beginning of this chapter, Winnie often accompanied her father when he traveled. It was during one of these trips that Winnie received the name Daughter of the Confederacy. Historians have noted that Winnie was an odd choice for this title. She had spent her formative years abroad. She hadn't really participated in the short-lived Confederacy. She was more fluent in German and French than in Southern "speak."

But it didn't seem to matter to southerners or Winnie. She willingly took her father's place when necessary. Davis was 56 when his daughter was born and 73 when she returned from Europe. Davis wasn't in the best health, and his daughter often substituted for him when he was unable to make public appearances.

Formed in June 1889, The United Confederate Veterans (UCV) was a merger of former confederate soldier groups that sprang up after the end of the Civil War. The veterans held annual reunions honoring former soldiers and Confederate leaders. They also wanted to preserve the idea of the Southern chivalry. Jefferson Davis and other top Confederate leaders often spoke at these events.

After the South's failure during the Civil War, these groups sought to bounce back by creating a new image. Not an image of defeat, but one of romanticized antebellum South, full of chivalrous southern gentlemen and genteel southern damsels.

"Representative southern women were literally placed on pedestals during veterans' reunions, to be worshipped by their knights," wrote Lee.[7]

---

7. Lee, 2014.

Winnie, in some ways, became more popular than her father. She was an icon for Confederate veteran groups *and* an inspiration for the United Daughters of the Confederacy. While her father was a symbol of the past, the veterans saw in her young, vibrant eyes a future for the South. In March 1891, the Missouri Daughters of the Confederacy elected Winnie as their president. This group later became part of the United Daughters of the Confederacy, an important association established in September 1894 in Nashville, Tennessee.

It was common to introduce young women (usually daughters of former Confederate leaders) during veterans meetings. Winnie was often the featured debutante. The attractive, educated, and unmarried women at these events represented the ideal southern women. They were told to wear white to these reunions to represent innocence and purity.

The United Daughters of the Confederacy lay a wreath at the Confederate Memorial during Confederate Memorial Day services at Arlington National Cemetery on June 5, 1922.

Many of the veterans hoped Winnie would marry the son of a Confederate leader like Robert E. Lee or Thomas "Stonewall" Jackson. They hoped a marriage alliance would preserve the Lost Cause bloodline.

Winnie had an active life outside of her travels with her father. The delicate social butterfly was a debutante in New Orleans. She traveled to New York and other cities — both northern and southern. She was well received wherever she traveled. Her every move was chronicled by papers both in the South and in northern cities.

Early writing career

Winnie wasn't just her father's traveling companion or an icon for the former Confederacy. She was also serious about her literary career. Winnie's first published work was an article about serpent myths, published in *North American Literary Review* (1888). The piece was a highly intelligent attempt to explain the origin of myths related to serpents (snakes).

She followed with a monograph of the Irish revolutionary Robert Emmet. Publisher John Lovell agreed to print the finished product, *An Irish Knight of the 19th Century,* in 1888. Davis earned about $300 (that's about $7,533.56 in 2018) from her first serious literary endeavor. The monograph went through three reprints. Each sold for $.25 each (about $6.28 in 2018).

Winnie published a second monograph, *"Foreign Education for American Girls"* in 1889. Although she was educated abroad, this work rallied against the education of American girls in foreign lands. She felt in doing so, it "... gives the pupil a different point of view from her own people and puts her out of harmony with her surroundings," wrote Ferrell.[8]

---

8. Ferrell, 1899.

Davis dabbled in poetry also. She had one of her poems published in the New Orleans Times-Democrat. She also belonged to a New Orleans literary club called the "Pangnostics."

Winnie falls in love

While visiting New York in the fall of 1886, Winnie met a young lawyer Alfred "Fred" Wilkinson, Jr. He was 28 years old, four years older than Winnie was at 22 years of age. All the young New York socialites considered him a catch. When he met Winnie, Fred became entranced by her Southern charm and beauty. They were so much in love they forgot their own name. But they had to keep the relationship hush-hush.

Fred's family tree was enviable by many. His paternal grandfather was one of the founders of Syracuse. When you shook the tree harder, Fred's maternal grandfather, Rev. Samuel Joseph May tumbled out. What's so bad about grandfather May? From a Southerner's perspective, he was a horrible man.

May was a well-known abolitionist. How could the daughter of the man who had fought so hard to rip the Union apart tell her father that she was in love with the grandson of a man who fought to end slavery? She couldn't. That's why they kept their love a secret.

In those days, the young couple didn't have social media or text messaging to keep in touch. But they managed to clandestinely meet and correspond. The two didn't care about their family's views on slavery. The Civil War wasn't *their* war. They were innocent tykes pulled into the fray by their families' opposing views.

The lovebirds spent a lot of time in New York. Between stolen moments of tender whispers and soft giggles, they hung out with journalist and publisher Joseph Pulitzer who was married to Kate Davis, Winnie's cousin.

One day in September 1888, Fred decided he would saunter on down to Beauvoir and ask for Winnie's hand in marriage. Davis famously responded: "Death would be preferable." [9] Today, we would probably label Davis as "extra." He would rather die than give his blessing for his daughter to marry a Yankee!

Although she loved Wilkinson and was legally old enough to marry without her father's permission, Winnie was first and foremost a dutiful Southern daughter. She wouldn't marry without her father's blessing. Her stomach knotted up with love for Fred, Winnie vowed to never love another man. Winnie was "extra" at times herself.

Davis eventually warmed up to Wilkinson. One of the reasons was his concern for Winnie's health once she was forbidden to marry her true love. According to accounts, Winnie suffered from an unnamed medical issue, often referred to as stomach ailments. Stress aggravated the condition.

Davis reminisced about the time when he was young and in love. He'd married Sarah Knox Taylor, against her father's wishes. Taylor was daughter of future United States president, Zachary Taylor. Unfortunately, Sarah died of malaria three months after the wedding. Davis was quoted saying that even after many years had passed he still swooned for his first wife.

---

9. Lee, 2014.

 Zachary Taylor was the 12th U.S. President. His term in office was brief. He serviced from March 1849 until his sudden death in July 1850.

Zachary Taylor

With these thoughts in mind, he decided to give his blessings to Winnie. The wedding was scheduled for the following winter. But the family told only a few close friends and family. What should have been a happy time was marred by tragedy. Because of the stress associated with the impending wedding, Winnie's health declined. Her parents sent her abroad to recuperate. The Pulitzers accompanied her.

Winnie arrived in Paris in October 1889. On December 6, Jefferson Davis died in New Orleans, Louisiana while his daughter was traveling. Winnie was distraught but unable to attend the funeral. Both her doctors and mother urged her not to make the trip because of her own shaky health. Today you could jet nonstop from Paris to Mississippi in about 10 hours. In the 1800s, traveling by sea took considerably longer.

Varina was concerned about her daughter's mental health. Winnie and the Pulitzers had journeyed from Paris to Italy. Varina enlisted Fred's help. He gladly made the trip overseas to check on his beloved.

According to reports, Winnie was depressed and heading for a nervous breakdown. She also seemed to have cooled on the idea of marriage. She was reluctant to set a firm date. This greatly troubled her mother, but Fred appeared unfazed.

Despite the dire circumstances, the couple apparently had a great time in Europe with the Pulitzers. But when Fred sailed for America in April 1890, the wedding date still hadn't been set. When Fred returned, Varina took matters into her own hands. She announced the pending nuptials.

When news of the engagement whispered in Southern ears, outrage spread like spicy high school gossip. The family received thinly-veiled threatening letters. The thought of a Southern belle marrying a northern Yankee was too much. Friends, family, and total strangers disapproved of the union. But not everyone shared this jaundiced view of the rivalry between the North and South. Some felt the marriage could signal a final reconciliation between the regions.

Fred received his share of hate mail. Unlike the letters received by the Davises, Fred's senders got straight to the point:

> "The very sleeping dead Southern soldiers would rise from their graves, and hustle you back to Yankeedom ere they would see the daughter of Jefferson Davis ruined, and shame-covered forever by marrying one whose only desire in marrying her is to get a Southern woman ..." [10]

10. Lee, 2014.

The writer promised he and his comrades would shoot Fred a thousand times through the heart before allowed him to marry the Daughter of the Confederacy.

Winnie tried to convince everyone to see her side. She reminded them that her future husband was only a child during the war. He wasn't responsible for his family's abolitionist views. He was a Syracuse lawyer, capable of supporting her. He was also an advocate of states' rights. This idea holds that individual states, not the federal government, should make, pass, and enforce laws, which was a view held by many Southerners.

October 1890. Wilkinson claimed it was health-related. Speculations flourished, including the Wilkinson's financial status, his ability as an attorney, and his family's past money problems. The so-called "Wilkinson affair" involved Alfred Sr.

The family patriarch's investment firm, Wilkinson Brothers, went belly up in 1884. Alfred Sr. and his brother, Forman, were accused of grand larceny. The brothers stole over half a million dollars from investors. The Wilkinson brood grew up wealthy. Fred's father had inherited a small fortune. He was also a successful stockbroker until the "Wilkinson Affair." Now the family fortune was depleted. Alfred Sr. slipped into alcoholism. He was likely saved from prison because he had political connections, but he didn't live long to enjoy his freedom. He died in July 1886.

The bank repossessed the family estate. Eventually, Fred purchased the property back. However, it was suspiciously torched in July 1890.

The reason for the breakup between the Romeo of the North and Juliet of the South (as they were sometimes called) appeared to be that of a dutiful daughter once again. Her mother was now opposed to the marriage, so it seems Winnie acquiesced again. Marriage wasn't in the cards for the young couple. Not only was the wedding canceled, but both remained unmarried.

 What ever happened to Fred? He had a successful career as a patent attorney. Fred died of coronary heart disease on May 27, 1918 in Atlantic City, New Jersey. He was 57.

New York state of mind

In 1891, both Varinas moved to New York to look for writing opportunities. They had unsuccessfully tried to get work in southern newspapers. Their decision was a wise choice. New York was a growing literary hub for aspiring wordsmiths. They quickly became a part of the New York literary scene.

Varina Howell Davis sits for a portrait painted by John Wood Dodge.

Both women started writing for the *Sunday World,* a newspaper owned by Joseph Pulitzer. He offered each $1,500-a-year salary. That's the equivalent of about $39,174.54 in 2018. Winnie penned short stories, sketches, poetry, and book reviews. Her mother wrote non-fiction pieces. The pair wrote for other magazines like *Ladies Home Journal.*

 Although Winnie spent most of her time after she moved to New York involved in literary pursuits, she still attended veteran's events as the Daughter of the Confederacy.

Although the mother-daughter duo often wrote for many of the same publications, Winnie had a solo writing career. She published the first of two novels in 1895.

The Veiled Doctor is out of print but a free Google e-book is available at **http://bit.ly/2DtheP6.**

Here are a few excerpts from the book:

"Ignorance he could forgive, vanity he might condone, but in his calendar of sins lying stood out supreme a red letter offence that burned into the very heart of affection and killed it root and branch."

"One of her good qualities was a genuine regard for children as long as they were not troublesome. In common with most pretty people she possessed no small attraction for them. This genius for making herself amusing to the little folk won her the only cordial friend she made in the old town a little six year old boy living next door who toddled back and forth on his chubby legs until he grew really puzzled as to which house he belonged."

"It had been raining, and although the sun was now shining, turning the dripping leaves to diamond edged jewels here inside the room it was damp and the atmosphere heavy with the odor of wet soot. In the black fireplace a great puddle of inky water had gathered."[11]

Winnie's second novel, *A Romance of Summer Seas* published in 1899, is also available online from Google Books: **http://bit.ly/2CWByrb.** Here are some excerpts:

"I looked at the woman from over my glasses to see if she knew what she was talking about and came to the conclusion that she did not."

"The ghostly night light only served to throw gigantic and distorted shadows on the walls and show Minerva's face and hands like white smudges in the darkness near the bed. The cicadas outside shrilled continually and occasionally, some belated carriage rolled through the street below, but otherwise there was nothing to distract my mind from the knot of troubles that bound us three together."

"The day we sailed was extremely hot and damp. Hong Kong steamed like a seething kettle and the low gray sky pressed down above it like a lid. In the houses the moisture ran down the walls in little streams and the coolies sheltered themselves in doorways and under balconies, dripping and disconsolate like fowls in a storm. It was the kind of day that made me feel as limp as a rag and as cross as a bear."[12]

Because the mother and daughter shared the same first and last name, publishing their work sometimes caused confusion. They found a solution.

---

11. Davis, 1895
12. Davis, 1899.

Winnie published under the name "Varina Anne Jefferson Davis." Her mother used the name "Varina Jefferson-Davis".

Varina Howell Davis' Literary Career.

Prior to her writing career in New York, Varina helped her husband finish his book, *A History of the Confederate States*, during the last year of his life. Davis had also started writing his memoirs before he died. After his death, Varina completed *Jefferson Davis, Ex-President of the Confederate States of America: A Memoir by His Wife*.

This photo of Winnie Davis' parents was taken in 1845.

Death, Legacy, and Recognition

Tragically, Winnie died young. She was only 34 when she died on September 18, 1898. The official cause of death was listed as "acute gastritis and gastroenteritis." Winnie died in Rhode Island, where she and her mother were spending the summer.

Always the dutiful daughter, Winnie had gone to Atlanta in July to substitute for her mother at a Confederate veterans reunion. Winnie didn't want to go. She had her own career as a blossoming writer. She was unmarried and childless. She could travel freely. But her mother insisted Winnie continue to preserve the Confederacy legacy. "Winnie's desire to please authority figures — her father before his death, her mother, and the southern war veterans who idolized her — was still strong," wrote Lee.[13]

Winnie was riding in an open carriage when it started raining. She was drenched but had to wear her wet clothes for several hours. She finally changed her clothes but the night wasn't over yet. She didn't have time to rest because she was scheduled to attend a ball later that evening. By the end of the night Winnie's health was sliding.

The next day Winnie boarded a train for Rhode Island. By the time she arrived, her health hadn't improved. She had a high fever. She had trouble eating and sleeping. Although she appeared to be vanishing before everyone's eyes, Winnie's doctor was convinced she would recover. She even had a few good days, leading her mother to believe the doctor was correct. Unfortunately, her health nosedived on September 17. The Daughter of the Confederacy died the following day.

---

13. Lee, 2014.

Varina was hysterical. She was to blame for her daughter's death, she cried. Winnie had told her mother she didn't want to travel to Atlanta, but Varina had insisted that she go.

Despite the official cause of Winnie's death, the actual reason remains a mystery. Heath Hardage Lee wrote that it is highly unlikely that Winnie died from getting wet in a rainstorm. "There must have been underlying physical and perhaps mental factors at play," she said.[14] Lee wonders if maybe Winnie picked up a bug during a recent trip to Egypt. Because Winnie frequently suffered from stomach ailments, it's possible her immune system was already weakened.

Winnie's family and close friends said goodbye to her at a small wake in New York. This was followed by a military funeral in Richmond on September 23. Winnie is buried next to her father in Richmond.

 Military funerals are normally reserved for veterans and active servicemen killed in the line of duty. Sometimes other prominent individuals (such as political figures) are honored with military funerals.

After Winnie's death, ownership of Beauvoir passed to her mother. But Varina had no interest in returning to the Gulf Coast. In 1902, she sold the estate to the Mississippi Division of the United Sons of Confederate Veterans. Varina Anne Jefferson-Davis died of pneumonia in New York on October 16, 1906.

Beauvoir was resurrected as the Jefferson Davis Soldiers' Home. The home provided shelter for veterans and Confederate widows. In addition to housing, there was a hospital, dining area, chapel, and graveyard.

---

14. Lee, 2014.

You can visit Beauvoir House today and see many of the Davis family's personal belongings. In August 2005, Hurricane Katrina ripped through Mississippi. Beauvoir was severely damaged, but some of the property has been rebuilt. The National Historic site contains a presidential library, museum, and home tour. Some of Winnie's artwork is on display at the site.

Perhaps author Heath Hardage Lee perfectly sums up who Winnie was. "Winnie was an original: a unique combination of intellectual and woman of the people, American and European, southern and northern."[15]

Although Winnie's name will forever be linked to the title Daughter of the Confederacy, she was also a talented wordsmith. She moved to New York to chase her literary dreams, and she made it. Winnie's life was cut short, but she left a small body of impressive work behind.

---

15. Lee, 2014.

Chapter Two

Amelia Bloomer

More Than a Fashion Namesake

A Family of Modest Means

According to Amelia Bloomer's husband, Dexter, the writer and women's rights activist's early life was "... devoid of any striking incidents." [16] Bloomer was born Amelia Jenks on May 27, 1818 in Homer, New York. She came from a family of modest means.

Her father, Ananias, was a clothier. That's a swanky way of saying he made or sold clothes. Her mother Lucy was highly religious and demanded the same spiritual zeal from her children. Amelia was the baby of the bunch, which consisted of four daughters and two sons.

"Her educational opportunities were limited to the district school of those early days. Then, it was commonly thought that about all a girl should be taught was to read and write, with a little grammar and less arithmetic," wrote Dexter Bloomer.[17]

---

16. Internet Archives, 2006.
17. Internet Archives, 2006.

Amelia Bloomer poses for a portrait in 1903.

Amelia had a short-lived teaching career, beginning when she was 17 years old. She taught for one term then moved to Waterloo, New York to live with her married sister, Elvira. She found a job as a live-in tutor for a couple of years.

Amelia met and fell in love with young Dexter Bloomer. On April 15, 1840, they said, "I do." She was 22; her groom was 24. Dexter was well educated. When he wed Amelia, he had already been a teacher and was studying law. He was an editor and entrepreneur. Bloomer encouraged his young bride to write for the *Seneca Falls County Courier*, a newspaper he co-owned.

FAST FACT When Bloomer married, the minister omitted the word "obey" from the normal wedding vows. Bloomer often alluded to this incident with satisfaction.

Dexter Bloomer had noticed Amelia's flair for writing from letters he received during their courtship. He wrote: "... she possessed the power of expressing her thoughts on paper with both ease and grace." [18]

Initially, she didn't want to write. She eventually agreed to write for the paper but only if she could do it anonymously. She often used the pen names "Gloriana" or "Eugene."

In 1843, the Bloomers became members of the Episcopal Church. Amelia was very active in the church. Because of her religious upbringing, she was a believer in Biblical scripture. However, around this time she started questioning some Bible passages. Specifically, she felt certain passages in the Bible, when correctly interpreted, "... elevated her to a joint companionship with her brother in the government and salvation of the race." [19] In other words, women and men had equal rights.

In reality, the law thought otherwise. This was particularly true for married women. Wives didn't have any rights until the middle of the 19th century. Married women couldn't own property or make contracts. Any money a wife earned belonged to her husband. Her children could be taken away without justification. When a wife's husband died, his property passed to his children not the spouse. Fortunately, many of these state laws were repealed. In New York, married women won property rights with the passage of legislation in 1846.

The repeal of these antiquated laws led to the women's rights movement. Bloomer became a part of the movement eventually, but her first fight was on behalf of temperance. The temperance movement encouraged abstaining from drinking alcohol.

18. Internet Archives, 2006.
19. Internet Archives, 2006.

The Temperance Reformation of 1840-41 started in Washington and eventually reached Seneca Falls, where the Bloomers resided. The movement encouraged former alcohol-swilling adults to "... abandon their drinking habits and become useful and sober citizens, while thousands more attached their name to the Temperance pledge of total abstinence from all intoxicating liquors," wrote Dexter Bloomer.[20] When The Ladies Temperance Society was organized in the Bloomers hometown of Seneca Falls, New York in 1848, Amelia enthusiastically became a member and an officer.

 Even before her marriage, Amelia was anti-alcohol. She even refused to have a glass of wine at her wedding.

In July 1848, the first women's rights convention was held in Seneca Falls. Prominent women's rights activists Elizabeth Cady Stanton and Lucretia Mott organized the event. Bloomer attended the inaugural event. During the convention, participants drafted a "Declaration of Sentiments." The document demanded basic rights for women, including property rights, rights relating to a woman's own children, a voice in government, and equal educational and employment opportunities.

Although Amelia attended the convention, she didn't sign the declaration. The Bloomers were swept up in the temperance movement at the time. They were active locally, and Amelia even wrote for the movement's newspaper, *The Water Bucket.*

---

20. Internet Archives, 2006.

The Lily

The ladies of the Seneca Falls Temperance Society decided they should have a paper dedicated to the Temperance movement. This idea became *Lily*, the first paper owned and operated by a female. But it almost didn't happen.

Amelia discussed the issue with her husband but instead of responding with enthusiasm, he threw cold water on the idea. He told Amelia the ladies didn't have a clue what it took to run a paper. For example, newspapers were expensive to print, he said. They could go into debt. Amelia relayed the message to her fellow auxiliary members but they were fired up and ready to go.

So, they moved forward with their plans. That fire in the ladies' bellies soon smoldered and then completely fizzled out. The women realized the project was too big of a commitment, but Amelia wasn't having it. They had already taken money from subscribers. They had secured a printer.

> "I could not so lightly throw off responsibility. Our word had gone to the public and we had considerable money on subscriptions. Besides the dishonesty of the thing, people would say it was 'just like women'; 'what more could you expect of them?' As editor of the paper, I threw myself into the work, assumed the entire responsibility, took the entire charge editorially and financially, and carried it successfully through," Amelia said.[21]

Amelia Bloomer wore many hats as she worked hard to churn out new issues of the bi-weekly *The Lily*. She was both editor and publisher. She prepared contracts, managed the subscription list, and wrote editorials and columns. She was the paper's proofreader. Her husband said she completed

---

21. Internet Archives, 2006.

each task "... heartily and earnestly." [22] The first issue's print run was about 300 copies. The number of subscribers steadily increased over time.

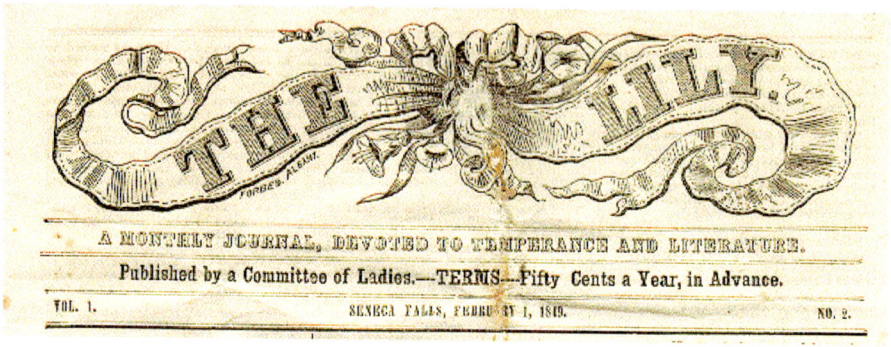

The Lily newspaper banner had a feminine style, depicting a sprawling bow-like title adorned with lilies.

Although the newspaper began as a temperance journal, the content soon changed. *The Lily* published recipes, moralistic pieces, and more. Women's rights, including suffrage (the right to vote), became a staple of the paper. Women's rights advocates, Elizabeth Cady Stanton and Susan B. Anthony, wrote many of the articles. Stanton wrote using the pseudonym "Sunflower." The earliest Stanton's articles dealt with the temperance, childbearing, and education. She soon focused on women's rights.

Amelia had a full life. Around this time, she was heavily involved in the local temperance campaign. She began giving speeches in New England. In addition to her temperance work, church activities, and publishing *The Lily*, she helped her husband at the Post Office. In the spring of 1849, Dexter Bloomer became postmaster, a position he held for four years. Amelia was his assistant, responsible for daily operation of the post office.

---

22. Internet Archives, 2006.

The Lily's masthead initially stated that a "committee of women" published the paper. That had been the plan. But when the women bailed on her, Amelia had taken on all the responsibilities with the exception of the few writers like Stanton who penned articles for the paper. So, beginning in 1850, she dropped this line from the masthead. From that point on only her name appeared as the publisher and editor. That same year, Bloomer introduced Stanton to Susan B. Anthony. The two became immediate friends and would go on to be recognized as the leaders of the women's rights movement.

 Amelia Bloomer never like the name "Lily". The society selected the name because they thought it was pretty. She would have changed the name once she controlled the publication but the paper became popular quickly. Amelia decided to keep the pretty name since subscribers were already used to it.

In the second year of *The Lily's* publication, the tone shifted. Temperance was still important and was covered aptly, but women's issues began to take up more space.

"... we see and hear so much that is calculated to keep our sex down and impress us with a conviction of our inferiority and helplessness, that we feel compelled to act on the defensive and stand for what we consider our just rights," Bloomer wrote. [23]

"Men make laws without consulting us, and of course they will make them all in their own favor, especially as we are powerless and cannot contend for our rights," she continued. [24]

---

23. Internet Archives, 2006.
24. Internet Archives, 2006.

Bloomer also voiced her opinion on women's suffrage and their right to have a voice in lawmaking. She was for suffrage but felt that these rights should come gradually. She also wrote about women's right to better education and to more work opportunities.

The Evolution of Bloomers

Many people are familiar with Amelia, though not because of her writing. The name "Bloomer" is associated with a popular style of dress that started in the 1850s.

In *The Lily*, Bloomer promoted a less restricted women's dress style while engaged in regular activities. It was hard for a woman during those days. Women normally wore layers of restrictive clothing.

The first layer was a snug corset

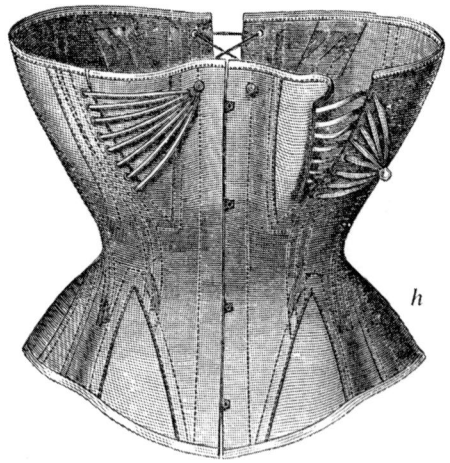

followed by a petticoat (or two or three)

and then finally her dress was added . . .

Yeah, that looks comfortable.

Bloomer suggested women should wear a style that featured a loose top and a skirt that stopped at the knee. To top off the ensemble, women would wear pants underneath. The idea took off and was christened the "Bloomer Costume" or more often simply "Bloomers".

The idea didn't originate with Amelia. She got the concept from temperance activist Elizabeth Smith Miller, who was also Elizabeth Cady Stanton's cousin. One day in 1851, Miller visited Bloomer wearing the outfit, and she liked the style so much she decided to wear it too. She then wrote about it in *The Lily*. And the rest — as they say — is history.

> Bloomer later stated, "As soon as it became known that I was wearing the new dress, letters came pouring in upon me by the hundreds from women all over the country making inquiries about the dress and asking for patterns — showing how ready and anxious women were to throw off the burden of long, heavy skirts." [25]

25. Biography.com, 2014.

Bloomer's endorsement of the new style helped bring women's dress reform to the forefront of the women's movement. So many women wanted to know about the style that she published sewing instructions in *The Lily.*

The style became popular, but not everyone liked the new costume. Women who dared to wear Bloomers faced taunts and ridicule. Although many women's rights leaders like Stanton and Anthony wore Bloomers initially, by 1853 they stopped. They felt the ridicule and attention was taking away from the women's movement's more important issues.

"At the outset, I had no idea of fully adopting the style; no thought of setting a fashion; no thought that my action would create an excitement throughout the civilized world, and give to the style my name and the credit due Mrs. Miller. This was all the work of the press," Bloomer once said.[26]

After the hoopla over the Bloomer costume, subscriptions soared. Circulation of *The Lily* rose from 500 to 4,000 per month.

Bloomer continued to wear the costume in public. She admitted that although it wasn't her idea she accepted that the style was linked to her. She also liked the costume, so it was easy to continue wearing it. She wore nothing but the costume for another six to eight years, she said.

"During this time I was to some extent in the lecture field, visiting in all the principal cities of the North and lecturing on temperance and woman suffrage; but at no time, on any occasion, alluding to my style of costume," she wrote.[27]

26. Internet Archives, 2006.
27. Internet Archives, 2006.

She said if people came out to hear her speak because of the costume that was okay. As long as her message was received, she didn't have a problem with being on display.

This photo is a depiction of Bloomer wearing the famous "Bloomer Costume" named after her.

The end of The Lily

The Bloomers moved from Seneca Falls to Mount Vernon, Ohio in late 1853. Amelia continued to publish *The Lily* and became assistant editor of the *Western Home Visitor,* a weekly paper owned by her husband, of which he was also editor. She became a member of the Ohio Woman's State-Temperance Society, where she served as corresponding secretary.

"It advocated temperance and sound morality, and its columns were filled weekly with matter appropriate to be read in the family circle," wrote Dexter Bloomer.[28]

Amelia wrote columns, some on temperance and women's fads. Many were about women's rights issues.

"All women need employment, active, useful employment; and if they do not have it, they sink down into a state of listlessness and insipidity and become enfeebled in health and prematurely old simply because denied this great want of their nature," she wrote in one column.[29]

The Lily continued to flourish, reaching about 6,000 subscribers. Amelia started writing more columns devoted to women's issues, although temperance was still her biggest concern.

"Where then shall the remedy for purifying and healing the nation be found? We answer, in the education and enfranchisement of woman! Loose the chains that bind her to the condition of a dependent, a slave to passion and the caprices of men. Open for her the doors of our colleges and universities and bid her enter. Hold

28. Internet Archives, 2006.
29. Internet Archives, 2006.

up before her a pattern for womanly greatness and excellence, and bid her to occupy the same high positions held by her brothers," she wrote. [30]

The couple decided to move again, this time to Council Bluffs, Iowa in 1855. Dexter Bloomer sold his interest in the paper. Amelia also decided to sell *The Lily.*

"There were no facilities for printing and mailing a paper with so large a circulation as mine, except a hand press and a stagecoach, and so it seemed best for me to part with the Lily. Finding a purchaser in Mrs. Mary A. Birdsall, of Richmond, Indiana, I disposed of the paper to her and it was removed to that city. Mrs. Birdsall published it for two or three years and then suffered it to go down, from what cause I never knew," Bloomer wrote.[31]

The Lily 2.0

The Washington Post resurrected *The Lily* online in 2017. The new version covers "national news, politics, gender equality, health, film, fashion, and more," according to their website.

A sample of recent articles include:

Babies behind bars: Children serve time with mothers in Mexico's prisons

McKayla Maroney sues USA Gymnastics, saying it tried to buy her silence on abuse

---

30. Internet Archives, 2006.
31. Internet Archives, 2006.

10 Latinas who dominated 2017

What inequities do women face in the workplace?

5 healthy food gifts for the holidays

California and Illinois must provide students free feminine hygiene products

Could 2018 be the year fashion becomes inclusive?

Will Meghan Markle really be the first mixed-race royal?

How men can be part of the #NotYouToo movement

After selling *The Lily*, Amelia spent more time on her original passion, temperance. She remained active in her church and lectured often. She didn't stop writing. She wrote for various newspapers, commenting on social and political issues. From 1851 until her death, according to Dexter Bloomer, Amelia was more involved in the women's suffragette movement. In 1870, she organized a women's suffragette society in Council Bluffs. She was the president of the chapter.

Although she wrote about and lectured on other issues, temperance remained Amelia's number one passion. Eventually this triggered a riff with other advocates. For example, while women like Stanton loudly spoke about important issues like the abolition of slavery, Amelia refused to speak publicly against the Fugitive Slave Act. This law mandated that escaped slaves be returned to their slave master if captured. After the Civil War began, women's rights issues were pushed to the background. Amelia then turned most of her attention to volunteer and community work.

The Bloomers didn't have any biological children. They adopted a brother and sister after moving to Council Bluffs. Not much is known about the siblings. The relationship between the parents and their adopted offspring appeared to have become strained and irreparable but little has been written about the reason for the estrangement.

Death, Legacy, and Recognition

In 1891, Bloomer experienced partial paralysis of her vocal cords. She was unable to speak for a short time. Although she regained her speech, it was, according to her husband, "... not so freely and readily as formerly."[32]

She also began to slow down. She was 73 years old, so it was completely understandable. Her husband wrote that her mind was still very much clear and her memory sharp as a shiny sword. He even joked that he was finally able to catch up with Amelia during their walks.

Her last trip was during the summer of 1894 when she went to Colorado Springs, Colorado, where she received treatment at a sanatorium. These medical facilities were popular destinations for the treatment of chronic illnesses.

She also visited her niece, who lived in northern Colorado. Amelia returned home in mid-August. She occasionally attended social events when she was feeling up to it. After Christmas, her health declined and she died December 30, 1894.

According to the local papers, Amelia Jenks Bloomer died of heart failure. She was 76.

---

32. Internet Archives, 2006.

Amelia Bloomer was the first woman to publish a newspaper. Following in her footstep are many female firsts in the publishing industry. Here are two examples:

- Josephine St. Pierre Ruffin was an African-American activist and journalist. From 1894-1897, Ruffin published and edited the newspaper, *Women's Era*. It was the first paper by and for African-American women.

- Nancy Hicks Maynard was a former reporter for the New York Post and the New York Times. In 1983, Maynard — along with her husband Robert — purchased the Oakland Tribune. They became the first African-American owners of a major daily newspaper. The couple published the paper until 1992.

Today we have numerous literary magazines and small presses founded or run by females, including:

- *Aunt Lute Books* (San Francisco, California)

- *Third World Press* (San Antonio, Texas)

- *421 Atlanta* (Atlanta, Georgia)

- *Sarabande Books* (Louisville, Kentucky)

- *Alice James Books* (Farmington, Maine)

- *The Feminist Press* (New York, New York)

 Amelia was the 1975 Iowa Women's Hall of Fame Honoree.

The Amelia Bloomer Project

Each year the Feminist Task Force of the Social Responsibilities Round Table creates a list of feminist books for young readers (birth to age 18). The task force is a part of the American Library Association. The Amelia Bloomer List began in 2002 and features fiction and non-fiction titles.

2017 selections include:

Non-fiction

Bessie Coleman: Trailblazing Pilot, by Carol Alexander

Maya Angelou, by Lisbeth Kaiser

Fiction

Two Friends: Susan B. Anthony and Frederick Douglass, by Dean Robbins

Girl in Pieces, by Kathleen Glasgow

When Susan met Stanton

Artist Ted Aub immortalized the historic introduction of Susan B. Anthony and Elizabeth Caddy Stanton by Bloomer. The statute features life-sized figures of Anthony, Caddy, and Bloomer. Aub revealed his work of art in 1999. It resides at the Women's Rights National Historic Park in Seneca Falls.

 The Bloomer's former house in Seneca Falls, known as the Amelia Bloomer House, was placed on the National Register of Historic Places in 1980.

Amelia Jenks Bloomer wore many hats during her lifetime: feminist, newspaper publisher, writer, temperance advocate, lecturer, and fashion reformer. She proved that a woman who was born of modest means could have an impact on generations of women (and men). Dexter Bloomer encouraged his wife to put pen to paper. Ultimately Amelia's talents brought her literary success.

Part II
Visual Artists

Visual arts are "the arts created primarily for visual perception, as drawing, graphics, painting, sculpture, and the decorative arts." [33] Visual artists often face the same barriers to advancement as writers. They may have to hone their craft while holding down a job. They create works of art and then wait with anticipation for someone to purchase their sculpture or painting.

Artists with exceptional talent often receive grants, fellowships, and other forms of financial support. These funds allow visual artists time and resources to pursue their passion. Between 1966 and 2016, the National Endowment for the Arts (NEA) provided $164.5 million for visual arts programs. According to a survey conducted by the NEA, "... visual arts is the second most commonly studied art form, after music, with nearly one-fifth of all American adults having taken visual art classes at some point in their lifetime." [34] The NEA supports not only visual artists, but also art teachers by offering professional development opportunities.

Famous male visual artists include household names like Vincent Van Gogh, Leonardo Da Vinci, and Pablo Picasso. The list of important female

---

33. Dictionary.com, 2017.
34. National Endowment for the Arts, 2017.

visual artists is long and exhaustive. They include sculptor Augusta Savage, painter Joan Mitchell, and photographer Annie Leibovitz. If you look closely, you'll probably find your local museum overflows with talented female visual artists.

(Left) Augusta Savage concentrates on the sculpture in front of her while Annie Liebovitz smiles at an event honoring her life's work as a famous photographer (Right).

Many visual artists start their careers when they are young, becoming successful as they age. Others wait until their golden years to begin their careers. Anna Mary Robertson Moses is one example. Affectionately known as "Grandma Moses", she began a successful career as a serious painter when she was in her late 70s. That's the great thing about becoming a visual artist. You can start at any age.

The second part of this book highlights two extraordinary female visual artists: Edmonia Lewis and Romaine Brooks. So, without further delay (drumroll, please), let's learn about these wonderful artists.

Chapter Three

Mary Edmonia Lewis

"Wildfire"

The Mysterious Mary Edmonia Lewis

There's a certain amount of mystery surrounding sculptor Mary Edmonia Lewis. She was believed to have been born in 1843, however, she claims she was born July 4, 1844. For a long time, the time and place of her death were also subject to speculation. Recent records indicate she died September 17, 1907. What we know for sure is Lewis was an extraordinary sculptor.

She was born Mary Edmonia Lewis in New York. Lewis was the first African-American and Native American sculptor to receive critical acclaim. She was known by her first name until around 1865, when she started using her middle name Edmonia. This was around the time she began her sculpting career.

Research suggests her mother, Catherine, wasn't a full-blooded Native American as Lewis claimed, but was of African-American and Ojibwa (Chippewa) descent. Her father, John Mike, was an escaped slave. Catherine was born in Canada.

Edmonia Lewis poses for a photo circa 1870.

Edmonia lived with her parents on the Credit River Reserve, which is now Mississauga, Ontario. When she was young, the family left Canada for financial reasons. The government paid Native-Americans living on reservations a yearly stipend. The money was based on the father's Native-American heritage. Since Catherine's father was African-American, the reservation council decided they wouldn't give the family a stipend.

The family then settled in New York. According to historical records, Catherine married an black man from Haiti whose last name was Lewis. No first name was recorded.

Lewis had a son named Samuel from his first marriage. Samuel was born in Haiti in 1835. He later moved with his parents to the United States.

 Edmonia's Chippewa name was "Wildfire;" Samuel's was "Sunflower".

The location of Lewis' birth is also a mystery. Some sources say she was born in Albany, New York; others list Greenbush or near Greenbush (both in New York). Still others simply report upstate New York. Ohio has been listed as a possible place of birth as well.

Both of Edmonia's parents died when she was young. Catherine's two sisters adopted the kids and moved them to Niagara Falls, New York.

They made items like baskets, blouses, and moccasins, which they sold to tourists. Young Samuel was an entrepreneur. When he was only 12, he became a barber.

The siblings lived with their family for four years. In 1852, Samuel developed "gold fever." When gold was discovered in California in 1848, hundreds of thousands of people from across the United States headed west. Samuel decided he would head to California to see if he could strike it rich. He left his sister in the care of Captain S. R. Mills.

Samuel sent money home to Mills for Edmonia's care. Samuel made money as a gold miner in California and opened a barbershop.

 Samuel eventually settled in Bozeman, Montana in 1868. He was a barber and real estate owner. Bozeman was only 4 years old when Samuel moved there. He was only one of 10 black residents. His home is on the National Register of Historic Places.

College bound

Samuel and a group of abolitionists worked to send Edmonia to college. In 1856, Edmonia enrolled at the New York Central College, a Baptist abolitionist school located in McGrawville. She remained at the school until 1858.

In 1859, Edmonia enrolled in Oberlin College in Oberlin, Ohio. She was about 15 at the time. She lived at the home of Reverend John Keep and his wife, until she left Oberlin in 1863. Keep was an abolitionist and on the board of Oberlin. What's interesting is that many of the African-American students boarded with white families. The city also had a growing community of African-American families. They also provided housing to the African-American students.

 Oberlin Collegiate Institute was founded in 1833 as an all-white technical and seminary school for men. In 1835, the school started accepting women and African-American students. This makes Oberlin the first coed, integrated college in the country.

Edmonia initially enrolled in the Young Ladies' Department at Oberlin (1859-1860). This preparatory department was designed to help students fill in educational gaps so they could succeed when they enrolled in regular college classes. After successfully completing coursework, the female students moved to the Young Ladies' Course (college courses) within the Young Ladies' Department.

Edmonia became interested in art while at Oberlin. Her earliest known surviving work is a pencil drawing of the muse Urania (1862).

Oberlin College's Allen Memorial Art Museum was founded in 1917.

In February 1862, Edmonia's time at Oberlin took a dark turn. She was charged with poisoning two of her white female friends. One was a student at Oberlin. She was accused of putting an aphrodisiac, known as "Spanish Fly," into glasses of wine. She then offered the wine to the young ladies, who were about to go on a double date.

Before the trial began, Edmonia was kidnapped, beaten, and left for dead in an empty field. Not only were the perpetrators never found, the authorities made no effort to investigate the crime.

The trial began on February 26. It was over on March 3. The defendant didn't take the stand during the trial. Edmonia's attorney was John Mercer Langston, an Oberlin alumnus. Mercer was also the school's fifth African-American graduate.

The trial ended with a 6-hour closing statement. The verdict? Not guilty. Langston won on the grounds of *corpus delicti*. This legal term means having substantial and irrefutable proof that a crime was committed. Because the prosecution hadn't saved the poisoned ladies' stomach or stool samples, there wasn't any proof the women were actually poisoned.

The trial over, Edmonia resumed her studies. In the spring of 1864 (with one term left before she could graduate), Edmonia experienced trouble once again. She was accused of theft. She allegedly pilfered art material from her teacher, Professor Couch. The charges were dropped because of insufficient evidence, but because of the two scandals, she was not allowed to enroll for her last semester. She was ineligible to graduate from Oberlin.

Professional Sculptor

Edmonia left Oberlin and moved to Boston. This is when she began her professional sculpting career. In Boston, Edmonia met many abolitionists including the famous William Lloyd Garrison, who introduced her to the sculptor Edward Brackett.

Brackett became Edmonia's teacher. She sold some of her work and then opened her own studio. She worked in clay and plaster. Many of her early subjects were famous Boston abolitionists, including Garrison and John Brown. Other subjects included Lincoln, Ulysses S. Grant, and Frederick Douglass.

Edmonia's first acclaimed work was created in 1864, a bust of Colonel Robert Shaw. Shaw was a Civil War hero who died while leading an all-black Massachusetts troop. Some of her work featured African-American, Native-American, and Catholic themes.

This is a stamped print of Edward Brackett.

This sculpture by Edmonia Lewis resides in the High Museum of Art
and is called "Columbus."

Although she was finding success as a sculptor, in 1865 Edmonia left Boston to take a teaching position in Richmond, Virginia, educating newly freed slaves. She lived in Richmond a short time before leaving the United States for Europe. In 1865, she settled in Rome, Italy where she met other expatriate artists living abroad. Edmonia was very famous in the United States and abroad. She remained in Europe for the rest of her life. Periodically she would return to the United States to exhibit and sell her work.

Harriet Hosmer

Harriet Hosmer was a Massachusetts sculptor who lived in Rome and was friends with Edmonia. Hosmer was one of only a few female sculptors to achieve financial success solely from her work. Commissioned pieces were created for the St. Louis Mercantile Library, the state of Missouri, and the city of San Francisco.

Hosmer eventually moved to England, while continuing to travel to Rome. She moved to hometown of Waterford, Massachusetts in 1900, where she remained until her death in 1908.

This is an engraving of Harriet Hosmer.

Famous works

Some of Edmonia's best-known surviving sculptures are:

The Arrow Maker: This 1866 piece shows a Native-American father teaching his young daughter how to make an arrow.

"The Arrow Maker" illustrates a line from the "Song of Hiawatha" by Henry Wadsworth Longfellow.

Moses (after Michelangelo): Completed in 1875, this piece is a copy of a sculpture created by the Michelangelo in 1515.

Edmonia's copies, like "Moses (after Michaelangelo)" were often sold to tourists.

The Death of Cleopatra: This famous piece was shown at the Philadelphia Exposition in 1876. It depicts the death of the Egyptian Queen Cleopatra. The sculpture didn't make the return trip to Italy with its creator. Edmonia couldn't afford the shipping cost of the massive two-ton sculpture. It was placed in storage and forgotten. It was rediscovered decades after Edmonia's death.

"The Death of Cleopatra" was carved in 1876.

Poor Cupid: In this 1876 piece, the mythical cherub Cupid reaches for a rose but instead gets hand caught in a trap.

"Poor Cupid" was modeled in 1872 and carved in 1876.

These pieces can be viewed at the Smithsonian American Art Museum in Washington, D.C.

Forever Free: This sculpture was created in 1867. It portrays the standing triumphant figure of a black male after the abolition of slavery. The piece also features a woman kneeling, believed to represent the man's wife. This piece is on display at Howard University Gallery of Art in Washington, D.C.

Death, Legacy, and Recognition

Edmonia's popularity eventually waned and people seemed to lose interest in her work. She disappeared and for a long time it was not known what happened to her. Edmonia never married and didn't have any children. There were reports that she may have died in 1909 or 1911.

In 2015, researcher Marilyn Richardson finally solved the mystery of Edmonia's death and located her final resting place. Using information from the 1901 census, Richardson determined that Edmonia relocated from Rome to London. Using this information, Richardson found Edmonia's will and burial records. Mary Edmonia Lewis died in Hammersmith Infirmary in London on September 17, 1907. Cause of death: Bright's disease, a chronic kidney ailment.

In recent years, interest in the mysterious Mary Edmonia Lewis has increased. Here are a few of the ways she's being honored:

- In April 2017, Rensselaer, New York resident Bobbie Reno, started a GoFundMe campaign to restore Lewis' gravesite in St. Mary's Cemetery in London. The campaign reached the $900 goal and subsequently Lewis' grave was restored.

- In 2017, Lewis was honored with a Google Doodle during Black History Month. The doodle depicted Lewis working on the Death of Cleopatra sculpture.

- Although ultimately she didn't graduate from Oberlin, the school has honored the famed sculptor. The Edmonia Lewis Center for Women and Transgender People is "... a collective of students, staff, and administrators who strive to transform existing systems of oppression based on sex, gender, race, class, sexuality, age, ability, size, religion, nationality, ethnicity, and language," according to center's website. [35]

- Tyehimba Jess, winner of the 2017 Pulitzer Prize for poetry, has a poem in his 2016 collection *Olio* written in Lewis' voice called "Minnehaha". The poem references an 1868 Lewis sculpture of the same name.

- "SEPIA SCULPTRESS: The Life and Trials of Edmonia Lewis" was a live performance on the life of Edmonia. The September 19, 2015 monologue was written and performed by Caroline Stephanie Clay at the Kennedy Center in Washington D.C.

Mysterious in life and even in death, Mary Edmonia Lewis didn't let obstacles thrown in her path stop her from achieving success as a visual artist. She lost her parents at a young age, but thankfully, she had an extended family that stepped in to raise "Wildfire" and her older brother. This same brother supported his little sister, making sure the doors of education swung open for her. Unfortunately, because of a string of bad luck, Edmonia wasn't able to complete her college career, but perhaps it was for the best. When Mary left Oberlin, she reinvented herself as Edmonia Lewis. Through hard work, perseverance, and great talent, she created some stunning sculptors. Hopefully, one day soon she'll get the recognition she deserves.

---

35. Edmonia Lewis Center, 2018.

Edmonia Lewis sits for a photograph circa 1870.

Chapter Four

Beatrice Romaine Goddard Brooks

No Pleasant Memories

Riches to Rags

You may have heard of someone going from rags to riches, from a poor life to one of plenty. The artist Romaine Brooks went from riches to rags, then back to riches again. She was born Beatrice Romaine Goddard in Rome, Italy on May 1, 1874, the last child of Ella Waterman Goddard and Major Henry Goddard.

Ella came from a wealthy family. Her father was Isaac Waterman Jr., a multi-millionaire who made money from salt mines in Salt Lake City and coal mines in Kingston, Pennsylvania. Henry Goddard was born in Providence, Rhode Island. His father was a famous preacher. Henry came from a family of furniture makers.

Henry was an alcoholic. Romaine's parents divorced before her first birthday. After the Goddard's divorce, Henry slipped deeper into his addiction and became an absentee father.

This photo of Romaine Brooks was taken circa 1894.

Romaine had two older siblings. Her brother, Henry St. Mar (called St. Mar), was mentally ill and the apple of Ella's eye. Romaine didn't talk much about sister Mary Aimée, known as Maya. Katherine, a third sibling died in infancy.

Ella suffered from mental illness. She bounced the family around from hotel to hotel and from country to country. Romaine's early childhood was spent in Europe. Ella was mentally and physically abusive to her young daughter. Ella dabbled in the occult, consulting mediums to "contact" the dead.

Romaine remembered her childhood as a "... court ruled over by a crazy queen." [36] Ella often dressed Romaine in duplications of clothes St. Mar wore when he was young. She told Romaine she wasn't as attractive as St. Mar. She once impulsively chopped Romaine's hair off with scissors.

In her book, *Romaine Brooks: A Life,* Cassandra Langer wrote, "Romaine was the last child of a disintegrating marriage, and her very existence served as a constant reminder to her mother of her failure in marriage." [37] Romaine later remarked she couldn't recall a single act of kindness from her mother.

When Romaine was 6 years old, Ella left her with Mrs. Hickey, "... an Irish washerwoman ... from the slums of New York City." [38]

Romaine was used to living a life of luxury. She was now living in poverty in the slums. While living with Mrs. Hickey, Romaine first began drawing — an activity her mother had forbidden. Her foster mom also introduced Romaine to an artist who lived nearby.

Ella continued to pay Mrs. Hickey for her laundry services and to take care of Romaine. Then one day Mrs. Hickey went to drop off Ella's laundry. Ella had left the hotel, leaving no forwarding address. She had returned to Europe to find a cure for her son's increasing erratic behavior, abandoning her daughter.

Romaine knew her grandfather's address in Philadelphia, but even though she was living like an urchin straight out of a Charles Dickens novel, she didn't want to return to her mother. She kept her lips closed about her grandfather.

---

36. Langer, 2015.
37. Ibid
38. Ibid

The family had to move to an even smaller apartment. There was only one bedroom and Mrs. Hickey's son, Mike, took it. Romaine slept in a bed with Mrs. Hickey and a female relative. "Romaine often went to bed hungry and rocked herself to sleep," wrote Langer. [39]

Romaine sold newspapers on the street to help her new family. Despite poverty and teasing from the neighborhood kids (they thought Romaine was fibbing about her family's wealth), Romaine didn't want to return to Ella.

Romaine's time with the Hickeys soon ended. Mrs. Hickey found out about Romaine's grandfather using her own detective work. Soon Romaine was whisked away to Philadelphia. Her grandparents sent Romaine to St. Mary's Hall, an Episcopal school in New Jersey. Romaine, now 8 years old, had previously been educated only sporadically.

At school, she became interested in reading and developed her drawing skills. Although the school was very religious and Romaine often got into trouble for what they considered inappropriate drawings (for example, devils and ghosts), she was happy.

Romaine's grandfather died in 1883. Her wealthy mother became wealthier — and possibly more eccentric. She still didn't claim her daughter. After four years at St. Mary's, Romaine was reunited with her mother, who was living in London. Her mother hadn't changed. St. Mar (now 19 years old) *had* changed — but not for the better. Romaine immediately noticed his frail body. St. Mar's shoulders were bowed. His hair and beard were in a tangled mess.

Soon Romaine was bouncing around Europe again. Ella's entourage included St. Mar, and a swinging door of Ella's boyfriends, servants, spiritual

---

39. Langer, 2015.

advisors, and doctors. When Romaine was 14 years old, her mother sent her to a convent school in Italy. She hated the school with its rigid rules. She hated her black and white convent uniform. She hated the convent's unappetizing food. But she was away from Ella. Around this time she began to develop what she called "crushes" on other girls, but she kept those feelings to herself.

Romaine was eventually expelled from the school after about two years. There are conflicting reasons cited for her expulsion. When she returned home, Ella told Romaine she had to continue wearing her convent dress.

Ella had purchased an extravagant Italian mansion, the Châteaux Grimaldi. The mansion was huge, containing 30 rooms. Romaine's quarters covered the entire top floor. She reportedly spent much of her lonely days filling notebooks with her artwork.

When she was 17 years old, Romaine's mother sent her to Mademoiselle Tavan's Private Finishing School for Young Ladies. The school was in Geneva, Switzerland, and although Romaine resented her mother's attempts to control her life, she was happy to get away from Ella.

Ella Goddard wanted her daughter to marry a rich man. Mademoiselle Tavan's was the type of school that instructed students how to act like proper young ladies. Students came from many countries including America, England, and Germany. Their classroom instruction didn't focus on the three R's (reading, 'riting, and 'rithmetic). The students were taught how to "... represent their husbands' interests rather than their own." [40]

While other young ladies filled their heads with thoughts of catching a rich husband, Romaine filled her notebooks with doodles and sketches.

---

40. Langler, 2015.

Romaine also had a decent singing voice. Her time in Geneva was a bust, so her mother decided to send her somewhere proper where she could nurture her singing and artistic skills. She sent Romaine to Neuilly-Sur-Seine in Paris to live with Monsieur and Madame Givend. Romaine remained with the Givends for a short time before deciding to declare her independence when she was 18 years old.

Independence

Using her small savings, Romaine found a room for rent. She quickly found a job as an artist's model. But Paris was too expensive and Romaine had to ask her mother for money. Ella eventually agreed to give Romaine a small monthly allowance. It wasn't a lot but it paid for Romaine's singing lessons and living expenses. She found a job singing at a café. But she didn't stay long. She didn't like the required costume. She felt humiliated, dancing "... a jig like a monkey," she said. [41]

Romaine next moved to a small village outside of Paris. A few months later, she moved to Rome to study art. She studied for free at the Scuola Nazionale during the day. She was the only female student. During the evenings, she took a sketching class at the Circolo Artistico. Romaine was one of four females in a class of 30 students.

The male students from Romaine's day class harassed her until she smacked one in the face with a book. They backed off but eventually returned to their juvenile behavior. One had the nerve to propose. She decided it would be a good time to leave Rome and spend the summer in Capri, Italy. This was the summer of 1898. Romaine was 24 years old.

---

41. Langer, 2015.

Romaine found inexpensive accommodations and blended in with the local artist community. Around this time, Romaine started selling her artwork. Her work was impressive, and she earned a reputation as a skilled portrait artist.

This painting is called "At the Seaside Self Portrait" by Romaine Brooks.

She made enough from the sale of her work to return to Paris in 1900 and enroll in the Académie Colarossi. This prestigious institution was one of the few Parisian art schools that accepted female students. Unfortunately, Romaine developed pneumonia and had to pause her studies. She recovered and returned in the fall of 1901.

That same year her brother, St. Mar, died. Romaine read about it in the newspapers. Romaine headed to Nice, France where she found her mother had erected a shrine to her dead son. She set a place for him at dinner. His clothes were still in the closet. She had pictures and busts of him scattered all over the house. "The once fastidious and fashionable Ella Waterman Goddard had turned into a depressed, slovenly old woman who wore an ill-fitting blond wig that kept slipping off her gray hair," wrote Cassandra Langer. [42]

Ella didn't last long after St. Mar's death. She died on November 1, 1902 of long-term untreated diabetes. Reportedly, on her deathbed, Ella asked Romaine for forgiveness. After her mother died, Romaine said she didn't feel any grief. "My mother was only a phenomenon I had been watching fearfully all my life. Death the climax nothing more," she said.[43]

Romaine inherited half the Waterman estate. Her sudden wealth included: six flats (apartments) in Nice and one each in Monte Carlo (Monaco), Dieppe (France), and Paris. She also inherited a chateau near Menton, along the French Riviera in France. She inherited furs, jewelry, clothes, shoes, gold and silver coins, and other goodies.

---

42. Langer, 2015.
43. Souhami, 2007.

Maya Goddard

Because Romaine didn't talk about her sister often, not much is known about their relationship. Maya married St. Mar's doctor, Alexander Phillips. Phillips had proposed to Ella but she turned him down. Phillips and Maya eloped to New York. The couple had two daughters: Ella Beatrice and Liliane. Her husband died seven years after the marriage. Maya then moved in with Ella. Later, she married the Compte de Valbranca, an Italian diplomat.

A Woman of Wealth

Romaine shared her good fortune with a few close friends. One was John Ellingham Brooks, an Englishman who was living in Capri. Brooks had proposed to Romaine the year before but she'd declined. Impulsively, she decided to marry him. The couple wed on June 13, 1903.

Was it a marriage of convenience? Romaine didn't want to be alone. She hoped being married would discourage men from bothering her. But what about Brooks? It was rumored that he wanted someone to take on his financial debts. He was also homosexual and wanted a wife who wouldn't interfere with his lifestyle.

His sexual orientation wasn't an issue with Romaine. Although Romaine would later spend the bulk of her adult years with writer Natalie Barney, at this point she'd had relationships with both men and women. Whatever the reasons, the marriage with Brooks lasted for less than a year. The two had different visions of what they expected from the marriage. Romaine was excited about traveling through England. She'd planned a walking trip. But her husband was more interested in social standing. He wanted to live in London and rub elbows with the elite.

Romaine decided to cut her hair in a boyish style. She bought hiking clothes for her planned backpacking sojourn. But Brooks said he couldn't be seen with her in public with her dressed the way she was and with *that* hairstyle. Romaine began to dislike everything about her new husband. She was especially concerned because he thought of her money as his. She finally fled when he suggested she make out her will "just in case."

She bought a studio in London and then sent word to her husband that she needed a quiet place to work. He followed her to London. He stalked her until she told him to leave her alone or she wouldn't support him. He retreated to Capri and lived on an allowance of £300 (about $1,400 a year; $37,300 in 2018). He remained on the island until he died of liver cancer in May 1929.

Portrait artist

In London, Romaine began to further develop her technique as a portrait artist. She traveled to Cornwall in the United Kingdom to study under the Newlyn Group. The group painted pastoral scenes. She rented a studio in St. Ives and studied with Stanhope and Elizabeth Forbes.

The students from the Forbes' class visited each other's studios and reviewed works in progress. Romaine placed her work on display for her fellow students to view. She was working on perfecting various shades of gray. When the students saw her little cardboards with nothing but gray, they were not impressed and left without uttering a word.

In 1905, Romaine bought an apartment in Paris on the right bank of the Seine River. She purchased a studio on the left bank. She became in demand by Parisians to have her paint their portrait. She also sketched a lot. She reportedly sketched all of her life but many of her notebooks didn't survive.

 Romaine was never associated with any particular style or art movement during her life.

Romaine's first solo exhibition was in 1910. She showcased 13 paintings at the prestigious gallery, Durand-Ruel. Most of the paintings were of women or young girls.

Romaine was known for her use of gray tones. She painted in gray, white, and black tones with hints of ochre, umber, and teal. This was "*artistic signature.*" She painted portraits of ordinary people and elite aristocrats of her time. Many of the women were dressed in androgynous or masculine clothing.

This painting by Brooks is called "Ida Rubinstein."

Shattered Dreams and a New Love

The solace Romaine found in Paris was shattered on June 18, 1914 when Archduke Franz Ferdinand of Austria was assassinated. His death ultimately lead to World War I. Everything changed for Parisians and Americans living abroad. Museums like the Louvre were closed. 9:00 p.m. curfews were imposed for women. Many of Romaine's friends fled Paris, but she chose to stay.

Although she opposed the war, Romaine volunteered for ambulance duty. Her efforts were short-lived. Romaine developed severe back pains from driving in an open car during the frigid winter, but she wasn't ready to abandon the cause. "She converted her cellar into a bomb shelter and stored her paintings in Bordeaux. Then she established a fund for wounded French artists," wrote Langer. [44]

 **FAST FACT** Romaine received the cross of the *Legion of Honor* in 1920, because of her contributions to the war effort. This esteemed award is the highest French honor given to individuals for outstanding military or civil service.

In the middle of the chaos of war, Romaine fell in love. Natalie Barney was a writer and heiress. Like Romaine, Natalie was an American living in Paris. They met in 1916 when Romaine was 42 years old and Natalie was two years younger. The women remained together for over 50 years. When Natalie met Romaine, she was already in love with a woman she met in 1909, Élisabeth de Gramont, called Lily.

Natalie was born in Dayton, Ohio. She was educated in New York City and France. When she was 33 years old, Natalie became a millionaire many times over, after the death of her father. She was known for hosting re-

---

44. Langer, 2015.

nowned literary salons. These festive gatherings allowed guests to schmooze and discuss great literature, art, and music. "Anyone who was anyone in French, Italian, American, or British circles attended, as did those in the arts from other countries," wrote Langer.[45]

Not willing to give up either woman, Natalie continued to see both. When the war ended in 1918, life returned to normal. Romaine appeared okay with the romantic situation but Lily — not so much. She threatened to leave Natalie. In June 1918, Natalie drafted a marriage contract to stop Lily from leaving. A year later, the couple honeymooned in the United States, leaving Romaine alone in Paris.

"How the three women resolved their conflicts is a mystery that remains. Romaine never wrote about the love triangle she chose to become involved in as a consequence of falling in love with Natalie," wrote Langer. [46]

The unconventional triangle lasted until Lily's death in 1954. During their many years together, each woman had her own separate apartments. They had dinner together weekly (usually on Sunday) at Natalie's house.

Romaine's status as a great artist continued to rise. She lived most of her life adult life abroad. She briefly lived in New York from 1935 to 1938. Returning to Paris, Romaine was met with a new threat: war. For the second time in her life, war loamed over Romaine's head like an ominous cloud.

Natalie was Jewish. There was a chance she could end up in a concentration camp. Romaine hatched a plan to flee with her love to Florence, Italy where she had previously purchased a villa. In June 1940, life changed for Romaine and Natalie. The threat of a Nazi invasion was quickly becoming

45. Langer, 2015.
46. Langer, 2015.

a reality. Their once carefree life in Paris was now overshadowed by "… constant threats of incarceration, Nazi occupation, food shortages, bombings, and the Allied invasion," wrote Langer. [47]

On June 14, the Germans invaded Paris, and the Nazi occupation was now a reality. For the first time, Romaine and Natalie lived together. It was a new experience, which lasted for six years. To complicate matters of living together, Romaine was showing some signs of the mental illness that haunted both her mother and brother. At the beginning of the war in 1940, 64-year-old Romaine exhibited paranoid and delusional behavior.

After the war ended in 1945, Natalie was anxious to return to Paris but Romaine wanted to remain in Italy. Natalie reunited with Lily, who had been trapped when the borders closed in June 1940.

The pair had a long-distance relationship with Natalie visiting Romaine in Florence and Nice. Romaine disappeared from the public eye and it's believed that she stopped painting (or decreased her output) at this time.

 Romaine wrote her memoirs, *No Pleasant Memories*, but was unable to find a publisher.

Famous Works

Romaine, like most artists, has a body of work she is most known for. Below are some of Romaine's most important and well-known portraits. The Smithsonian Museum owns them all. Romaine began gifting some of her work to the museum beginning in 1966.

---

47. Langer, 2015.

Self–Portrait: This is probably one of Romaine's most famous works. The 1923 self-portrait is a haunting window into the soul of the artist. Present are Romaine's artistic signatures. Romaine wears a man's top black top hat and black tailored suit. Her face is painted powdery white, her lips a stark red. The brim of the top hat shadows her eyes. Gray gloves envelope her hands.

Self-Portrait by Romaine Brooks

*Le Trajet (*The Path, 1911): This oil on canvas piece depicts a relaxed nude Ida Rubinstein, who appears to float on a winged cloud against a dark background.

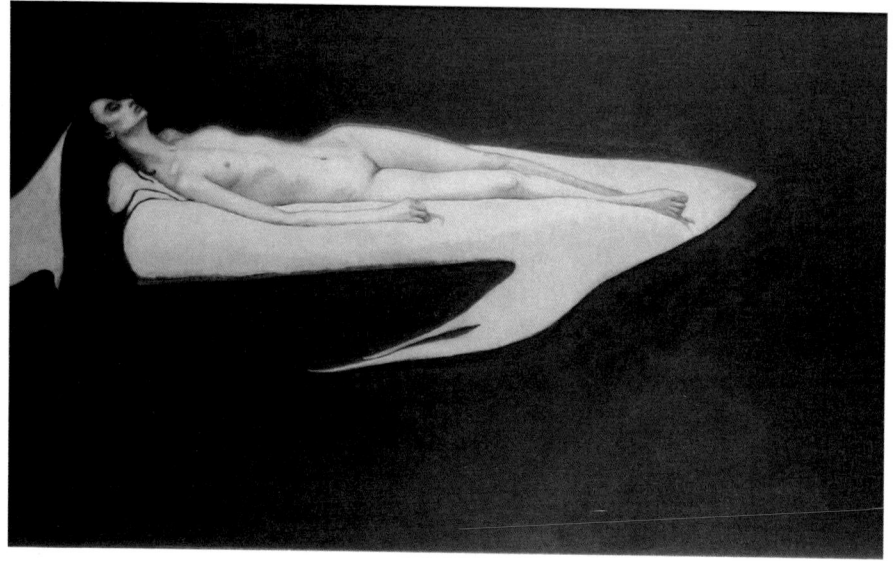

Le Trajet by Romaine Brooks.

Azalées Blanches (White Azaleas): This 1910 work was featured in Romaine's first solo exhibition. It is also one of her first female nude paintings. Although male artists during Romaine's time often had nude females as subjects, it was unusual for a female artist to have the same.

Una, Lady Troubridge: This 1924 portrait features British aristocrat, translator, and writer Una Troubridge and her two dachshunds. Like Romaine's self-portrait, Una is dressed in tailored men's clothing. She sports a short bobbed hairstyle, and a monocle dangles from her eye.

Peter, (a Young English Girl, 1923-1924): The "Peter" in this portrait is British painter Hanna Gluckstein. She chose the gender-neutral professional name "Gluck" in the early 1920s. Later she used the name Peter

Gluck. Gluck always dressed in men's suits and hats. Romaine perfectly captures Gluck's androgyny in this portrait.

La France Croisée: This is another portrait featuring Ida Rubinstein. The 1914 work shows Rubinstein in a nurse's uniform. A large red cross punctuates her black cloak. In the background, the city of Ypres (in Belgium) burns. The nurse gazes sternly ahead, a white scarf on her head blowing in the wind. The portrait was in response to Romaine's opposition to World War I. Reproductions of the piece supported the Red Cross efforts.

La France Croisée by Romaine Brooks.

Final portrait

In 1961, at the age of 86, Romaine painted one last portrait. Her eyesight had started to fail and she hadn't painted for a long time. The subject was an Italian nobleman named Uberto Strozzi. Romaine had been friends with Strozzi since they met in Italy during World War II. Romaine's signature grey tones are still vividly present. In the portrait, Strozzi sits in profile, slumped in a black chair. His gray suit almost blurs into the portrait's gray background.

Death and Legacy

In 1967, 93-year-old Romaine settled in Nice, where she remained until her death. Romaine and Natalie's relationship had become strained but they continued to see each other for a while. The tension began when Natalie started a new relationship with Janine Lahovary, who was 20 years younger.

The last year of Romaine's life, she didn't communicate with Natalie at all. She died December 7, 1970, alone in her apartment with only her servants to comfort her. She was buried in Nice next to her brother, St. Mar.

Because of Natalie's own frail health, Janine didn't tell her of Romaine's death until three months later. Natalie died 18 months after Romaine on February 2, 1972. She was buried with a picture of Romaine.

 Both Romaine and Natalie died at the age of 96.

Romaine's greatest contribution to the art is her view of the women in her portraits as subjects rather than objects. Her androgynous style of dress — both in her own clothing selection and in that of her subjects' — is still prevalent today. Gender identity fluidity is not a new concept, but Romaine and many of her friends were probably among the first group of gender non-conformists to be recognized as such.

In her article, "Meet Romaine Brooks, A 20th Century Artist Who Paved The Way for The 21st Century Lesbian," Pricilla Frank wrote, Romaine changed the history of art and gender equality with a simple brushstroke. Perhaps that is Romaine's true legacy. [48]

---

48. Frank, 2017.

Part III
Performing Artists

The U.S. Copyright Office defines performing arts as "... works that are intended to be performed for an audience." [49]

This includes a range of art forms including opera, ballet, spoken word poetry, performance art, and stand-up comedy.

Some performing artists are classically trained, like ballerinas. Others are born with the natural ability to sing with perfect pitch. These artists perform in front of sell-out crowds or dance in the subway for tips. That's the great thing about the performing arts — entertainers can perform just about anywhere.

Most performing artists focus on one discipline. Others might be referred to as a "triple threat" — they can sing, dance, *and* act. One of the artists highlighted here, Hattie McDaniel, was a triple threat.

This field is so popular that there are entire schools dedicated to the performing arts. For example, in New Orleans, the New Orleans Center for

---

49. U.S. Copyright Office, 2018.

Creative Arts (NOCCA) offers talented high school students the opportunity to hone their craft. The school has turned out many great artists including Harry Connick, Jr., Anthony Mackie, and Wendell Pierce. Most major cities, like New York City, have performing arts schools.

Our last section features women in the performing arts. These women excelled in dance, music, and television. Let's take a look at these extraordinary, dedicated, and passionate women.

Chapter Five

Carmen Amaya

Queen of the Gypsies

Queen of the Gypsies

Carmen Amaya was a flamenco dancer — but not just *any* flamenco dancer. She has been called the greatest flamenco dancer ever and "Queen of the Gypsies." Flamenco is a rhythmic style of dance made popular by Spanish gypsies. Traditional flamenco dance is made of three parts:

Cante (voice)

Baile (dance)

Toque (guitar)

A fourth component, Jaleo, includes audience participation such as foot stomping and hand clapping.

Carmen was born November 2, 1913. Her birthday coincides with the Mexican holiday *El Dia de los Muertos* (The Day of the Dead). This is the accepted date, although her exact year of birth is unclear. She may have been born in 1918, according to information from the 1930 census.

Carmen came from a family of talented artists. Her mother, Micaela Amaya, was a dancer; José Amaya, her father, was a gifted guitarist; her maternal grandfather, Juan Amaya Jiménez, was also a skilled dancer.

Carmen was born during a rainstorm in Somorrostro, a gypsy *barrio* (neighborhood) in Barcelona, Spain. At birth she was described as a "... girl, dark and very small, with a large mouth and closed eyes and she greets the world with a brazen cry." [50]

In his book, *Queen of the Gypsies: The Life and Legend of Carmen Amaya (1999),* Paco Sevilla writes that Carmen Amaya was "... *gitana de los cuatro costaos*, pure gypsy on all sides, and clearly a true child of the bronze-skinned gypsies who had wandered into Spain from India centuries earlier." [51]

Carmen was one of 11 children. Five siblings died at birth or in infancy. Surviving siblings were two brothers (Paco and Antonio) and two sisters (Leonor and Maria). Carmen spent her childhood at the beach, dancing to the beat of the waves. She played with shells and rocks for toys. She sometimes made baskets. One of her "chores" as a child was fetching water from a local fountain in Barcelona where she would stand with her pot in a "... long line of dirty children — children who are lice-ridden, starving, and cruel." [52]

Carmen began dancing almost as soon as she could walk. By the time she was three or four years old, she knew how to dance the gypsy dance, the *baile gitano.*

 **FAST FACT**   Female flamenco dancers are called *bailaora.*

50. Sevilla, 1999.
51. Ibid
52. Ibid

When Carmen was a child, her father started taking her out with him at night to earn money. He strummed his guitar while Carmen danced. He took the bare-footed child into bars and cafés. With tips earned, he would buy food for the family.

The duo became very popular. Many local establishments requested the father-daughter pair to perform. But they had to be careful. A guard would sometimes throw the two out of the bars because of Carmen's age.

When Carmen was 10 years old, she danced at the popular Bar de Manquet in Barrio Chino. Local dockworkers and gypsies hung out at the bar. It was *the* place to listen to flamenco music and watch flamenco dancers. Carmen took the stage name "*La Capitana*" (the Captain). She danced with her aunt, Juana la Faraona, while her grandfather and father played guitar.

 Carmen never had any formal training. She soaked up what she observed like an eager sponge.

In 1925, when Carmen was 12 years old, she and her father traveled to Madrid to perform at the Palacio de la Música. The gig lasted only 10 days because the director of the café disappeared. The father-daughter team returned to Barcelona and to their regular routine.

Shortly after her return home, Carmen was asked to tour with Manuel Vallejo. He was a flamenco singing *payo* (not a gypsy). Carmen's popularity was spreading by word of mouth. Many great flamenco musicians and dancers wanted to perform with her. Young Carmen was so popular she danced for the Spanish monarch, King Alfonso XIII. In 1929, Carmen had her first French performance thanks to the dancer Vincente Escudero.

International Fame

By age 16, Carmen had been dancing professionally for over 10 years. Throughout her career, Carmen usually danced in pants and was often criticized for doing so. She normally wore high-waisted black or white pants with a matching vest and white shirt.

In her routines, she used fancy footwork typical of male dancers. She said the reason for wearing pants was simple: spectators couldn't see her feet if she was wearing a long traditional dress. Carmen put a lot of effort into her footwork and she wanted people to see her feet.

 Carmen was tiny. Her height as an adult was just 4 feet 10 inches and she weighed about 90 pounds.

Carmen danced throughout Spain. She performed in Paris, Berlin, and Nice. She thrilled audiences in Lisbon and in Buenos Aires. She appeared before sold out crowds in Argentina, Uruguay, and Mexico. Large crowds in Brazil, Colombia, and Venezuela welcomed her. During the Spanish Civil War, Carmen traveled extensively, growing in popularity.

Her dances were improvisational. Each dance was slightly different each time. When describing how she prepared for a performance, she said, "I let myself be carried by the music and I dance what comes out. I know how to begin the dance and how to end it. But I don't know what happens in the middle!" [53]

---

53. Sevilla, 1999.

Spanish Civil War, July 1936 – April 1939

The Spanish Civil War was fought between the rebels (called Nationalists) and the Spanish Republic. General Francisco Franco, who attempted to seize control of the Spain, led the rebels. Many groups, including communists, aided the government. Franco and his troops received aid from Germany and Italy.

People from other countries volunteered to fight against Franco. This included volunteers from the United States, France, and Britain. They often fought even though their governments ordered them not to get involved. These groups were called International Brigades.

The rebels eventually won the war when the last Republican troops surrendered on April 1, 1939. Franco became Spain's new ruler, remaining in power until his death in 1975.

U.S. Tour

Carmen's first U.S. tour was in New York in 1941. Her original contract called for 25 days of performance. She would receive payment of $15,000 — about $251,703.06 in 2018.

According to a report in *Time* magazine published after her first show, the contract stipulated payment of $1,000 a week ($16,780.20 in 2018) and a percentage of the ticket sales (about $2,000 a week; $33,560.41 in 2018).

Carmen's appearance was a success. Popular magazines like *Newsweek* and *Life* raved about her stunning performances. President Franklin Roosevelt invited Carmen to perform at the White House. She agreed but refused to take payment. She told Roosevelt, "I want to say thank you to the man who governs this country that has given me much more than I deserve." [54]

---

54. Sevilla, 1999.

After her White House appearance, the president sent Carmen a gift. It was an expensive jacket embroidered with stones, gold, and diamonds. Carmen was generous and often shared her gifts with members of her troupe. When she received the jacket, she removed the jewels and shared with her company. They made jewelry from the precious stones.

 While visiting New York, the police department and the U.S. Marines made Carmen an honorary captain.

Carmen's increasing wealth allowed her to purchase homes in New York, Hollywood, and Argentina. But she didn't dress elaborately, so it was often hard to tell she was wealthy. One incident of judging a book by its cover happened when she was in New York. Carmen was walking down Fifth Avenue when she spotted a fur in a shop window. The salesgirl didn't think the gypsy could afford the expensive coat. Carmen gave the clerk the stink eye.

Carmen reportedly threw a fat stack of cash on the counter. This has been widely reported. Accounts vary on the number of furs she purchased. She may have bought from three to seven. She kept one for herself and gifted the others to women in her troupe.

 Carmen didn't eat much but loved to drink strong, black coffee.

Carmen was a great dancer, but she could also sing. Because of her popularity, Carmen received a two-album contract from Decca Records in 1941. She completed the first in June. It took only six days to record 15 songs.

Most great artists long to perform at Carnegie Hall. Carmen was no exception. She made her debut on January 13, 1942. The concert was a success, although one writer, John Martin of the New York Times, felt the venue was too big to appreciate Carmen's talent. "Amaya needs a small and informal frame with as little division as possible between herself and her audience," he wrote. [55]

After a few more performances in New York, Carmen had tour dates across the United States. She performed in Detroit, Michigan; Chicago, Illinois; Seattle and Tacoma, Washington; San Francisco, Los Angeles, and San Diego, California; Princeton, New Jersey; and Philadelphia, Pennsylvania.

On May 17, Carmen returned to Carnegie Hall. In the fall, the troupe was on the road again. They visited many of the cities from the previous tour, adding new stops like Portland, Oregon. The troupe even crossed the border, performing in Winnipeg, Canada.

In December, Carmen performed for the third time within a year at Carnegie Hall. She continued to perform in New York and other cities. In August 1943, she performed at the Hollywood Bowl in California.

Things were going fine, and then tragedy struck. Carmen's father died of throat cancer in 1946. The family patriarch had been the troupe's manager. Her brother, Paco, took over business negotiations. By this time, Carmen was an international star with many contract offers. She had to turn some down because of her busy schedule.

In early 1947, the tribe returned to Madrid. Carmen and her company immediately began performing in Spain. She still had some Hollywood contracts left to fulfill. But first, she was off to Paris for a performance in April 1948 at the famed Théâtre des Champs Elysées.

---

55. Sevilla, 1999.

 Carmen appeared as a dancer in 11 movies. Her first appearance was in *Juan Simon's Daughter* (1935). Her last movie was *Los Tarantos* (1963).

Several non-family members were added to Carmen's company over time. One of the new members was guitarist Juan Antonio Agüero. Many of the dates on Carmen's historical timeline aren't exact. It's believed Juan Antonio joined the group between 1947 and 1951.

One night, Juan Antonio surprised Carmen by asking: "*A que no casaria usted conmigo?*" ("Why don't you marry me?") Carmen thought he was joking but when she looked into his eyes, she realized he wasn't. She wondered if she could marry him. He was not a gypsy. He was also 14 years younger. Surprisingly, Carmen said yes. She had contracts in France and Barcelona to fill first.

The couple married at 6 a.m. on October 19, 1951. The wedding was kept secret to avoid press coverage. The newlyweds didn't take time off for a honeymoon because they had scheduled performances, including one that same night. The Amaya troupe continued performing throughout Europe, in Argentina, and in Africa.

 Just before her marriage, Carmen returned to her childhood home. It was her first visit in 15 years. TV crews were on hand to record her visit. As she walked through the streets searching for her familiar sites, people poured from their homes to see the legend. Somorrostro is now a beach. A fountain named in Carmen's honor is located next to the beach.

After touring in South America and Mexico, Carmen returned to New York in September 1955. There were a few changes. Some of her family members had left the ensemble. Her husband was trying to wiggle financial control of the company from Carmen's brother, Paco. He thought he could better manage the business.

In New York, Carmen performed four concerts at Carnegie Hall. She received a lot of praise for her performances. The company then performed at a few venues in the east before returning for additional concerts in New York in November. From there, they traveled to Hollywood, spending two weeks before closing out 1955 with a New Year's Eve performance at Huntington Hartford Theater.

Decca Records offered Carmen another recording deal while she was in New York. The result was *Queen of the Gypsies: The Rhythms of Carmen Amaya.* The recording is considered a classic.

During the next few years, Carmen continued tours across the United States, Canada, Mexico, Central America, Paris, Spain, and Cuba. The venues ranged from small intimate restaurants to huge civic center concerts. New members continued to come and go. Her brother Paco eventually left the company.

In 1959, while visiting Barcelona for the dedication of a fountain named in her honor (*Fuente Carmen Amaya*), Carmen fell in love with a house in the small Spanish town of Begur, located 60 miles north of Barcelona. She purchased the house and made some renovations, but didn't have much time to enjoy it because of her hectic schedule.

Traveling Gypsies

Although the traveling band of performers and family members stayed in some of the best hotels, they were often asked to leave. The family liked to cook in their room. They also behaved inappropriately.

According to one report from their stay in Paris: "The neighbors in the adjacent hotel rooms are frightened. The doors that lead to the hallways are always open; the children never stop yelling; the men strum their guitars; the women sing while they sew and suckle their children. The floors are strewn with rags, the beds are unmade, and the floor is invaded by the strong odor of fried sardines, pepper [sic] omelettes, and stew."[56] This reaction was typical of the discrimination gypsies faced. Because of their nomadic lifestyle, they were often thought of as nothing more than a traveling band of thieves and beggars. They were stereotyped as uneducated, boisterous, and dirty.

Carmen returned to the United States in early 1961. Her ensemble was smaller but her performances were grand. After performing in America, Carmen headed to Mexico. In 1962, while on tour in Mexico, Carmen had to cut her trip short. She was filming the movie *Los Tarantos* in Spain. She was also having a lot of back problems. Carmen would perform and then have to rest in bed after each show. While filming, she also had to take time off to rest.

Carmen had been cast in the role because the director wanted an authentic gypsy dancer to play the mother of the lead character Rafael Taranto. He also thought her name would draw crowds to the movie theaters. Carmen was scheduled to shoot a few scenes but her performance was so outstanding, they decided to add additional scenes and dialogue for her.

---

56. Sevilla, 1999.

Death and Legacy

When she finished filming, Carmen returned to her tour. Her back pain was severe. Juan Antonio begged Carmen to see a doctor. "After the next stop," she promised. But after the next stop, she delayed seeing a doctor. Eventually the pain became so severe, she couldn't go on.

The doctor delivered a crushing blow. He advised Carmen to stop dancing. But she refused. Dancing was her life, she said, so she kept up her grueling schedule including return engagements to New York in May 1962.

In 1963, she returned to her home in Begur after collapsing during the middle of a tour. She didn't protest seeing a doctor this time. He prescribed the same treatment as the previous doctor: complete rest.

Initially she rested. She spent time gazing out at the Mediterranean Sea. But she was anxious to dance again. Soon she got the chance. There was a fundraiser to solicit money to light the Begur castle. Carmen loved the castle. She could see it from her window. She offered to dance at the event.

The fundraiser was a success. But after the performance, Carmen collapsed. She agreed to undergo comprehensive medical tests in Madrid. The doctors again recommended rest. Carmen and Juan Antonio returned to Barcelona.

Carmen was eventually diagnosed with kidney disease. She remained at a hotel in Barcelona for a short time. In early November 1963, she returned to Begur. Her health was declining. On November 12, she asked for last rites from her priest. As news spread of Carmen's impending death, family members, friends, and fans flocked to Begur.

On November 13, the governor of Spain traveled to Begur to present Carmen with the highest civilian award, the *Lazo de Dama de la Orden de*

Isabel la Católica (Loop of the Order of Isabella the Catholic). This award recognizes an individual's outstanding contributions to the Spanish culture. On November 15, the city of Barcelona gave Carmen the Medal of the City.

Carmen's health deteriorated. She couldn't eat. She was frail and emaciated with sunken dark eyes. On November 19, 1963, Carmen Amaya died, less than a month after her birthday. In Paco Sevilla's book, he wrote that Carmen once said she would die if she couldn't dance. "When it was absolutely certain that she would never dance again, she died," he said.[57]

According to official reports, Carmen was lucid until she took her last breath. She died holding her husband's hand, surrounded by her doctors and a priest.

Thousands poured into the city to pay their respects to the great dancer. She was buried in a mahogany coffin, dressed in white. She had a white *mantilla* draped over her face. Her hands hugged rosary beads.

 A *mantilla* is a lace or silk veil worn by women in Spain.

The city honored Carmen by flying flags at hast-mast. Windows and balconies were covered in black. The lights in the castle remained on continuously. Workers toiled through the night to prepare a tomb for Carmen's burial. The city donated a parcel of land for Carmen's final resting place.

On November 20, the small town shut down as everyone attended Carmen's funeral. Her casket was carried first by her husband and other family members. Then it was passed on to some of the older gypsies, then a group

---

57. Sevilla, 1999.

of younger gypsies. Finally, a group of neighbors and friends carried her remains. It took two hours for the procession to reach the church from Carmen's house. The crowd was too large to fit inside the tiny chapel. Most had to wait outside during the funeral.

 Eventually Carmen's remains were moved to Santander where Juan Antonio was born. Juan Antonio married again three years after Carmen's death. He fathered two children with his second wife.

Carmen's greatest gift to the world was infusing passion and fire into flamenco dancing. She was such a talented dancer that she didn't rehearse her parts. Flamenco singer Domingo Alvarado, who performed with Carmen at Carnegie Hall in 1958, asked her about rehearsing. She told him to sing and she would dance to his singing.

Carmen was widely loved for her dancing ability but she was also an overall nice person. Dancer Luisa Triana's father Antonio performed with Carmen from 1940-1943. She described Carmen as ". . . an extraordinary being, but never pretentious."[58]

"To see Carmen in person would touch your soul. She used her technique to "create art", the musicality of her feet would transport you to another level, it was pure creation, each show had its magic, her alegrías couldn't be matched, and audiences never wanted it to end, things that weren't captured on film. That's why any flamenco fan who never saw her perform live, can't understand how important she really was," Triana said.[59]

Carmen has also been honored with several streets named for her. This includes streets in Buenos Aires, Barcelona, Begur, and L'Hospitalet de Llo-

---

58. Zatana, 2013.
59. Zatana, 2013.

bregat (in Catalonia, Spain). There's a plaza named after her in Cornellà de Llobregat (also in Catalonia). Other homages to Carmen include statues of her in the Jardins de Joan Brossa on Montjuïc and Begur. The El Tablao de Carmen, a flamenco venue, is also named after the dance sensation.

This is a sculpture honoring Carmen Amaya by Josep Cañas.

Chapter Six

Maria Tallchief

Prima Ballerina

Betty Marie

When Elizabeth Marie Tall Chief was a young girl, she thought her father owned their town. "He had property everywhere," she said.[60] "The local movie theater on Main Street, and the pool hall opposite, belonged to him. Our ten-room, terra-cotta-brick house stood high on a hill overlooking the reservation."[61]

Her father, Alexander Joseph Tall Chief, didn't own the town, but his family lived comfortably. Tall Chief was a full-blooded Osage American Indian. When her father was a young boy, oil was discovered on tribal land. Overnight the tribe became rich.

Maria grew up on the Osage reservation in Fairfax, Oklahoma. Her father's first wife was a German immigrant. They had three children — Alexander, Tommy, and Frances. Their mother died when the kids were young.

60. Tallchief, 1997.
61. Tallchief, 1997.

Maria's mother, Ruth Porter, came to Fairfax to visit her sister. Her sister worked as a cook and housekeeper for Maria's grandmother. Porter was instantly attracted to Alexander Tall Chief.

Porter was born in Oxford, Kansas. According to Maria, her mother was "A determined woman of Scots-Irish blood . . . beautiful, with light brown hair, gray eyes, and delicate features."[62]

The two soon married. The children from the first marriage went to live with Maria's grandmother. Maria was born on January 24, 1925. She was named after her grandmothers, Eliza Tall Chief and Marie Antoinette Porter. Maria was called Betty Marie as a child. Later she adopted Maria Tallchief as her professional name. Maria's sister Marjorie was born 21 months after her.

Maria received her first ballet lesson when she was three. During the summer, the family often drove to Colorado Springs, Colorado. While Mr. Tall Chief played golf, the ladies splashed in the pool at the Broadmoor Hotel. Maria's first ballet lesson was in the hotel's basement.

"What I remember most is that the ballet teacher told me to stand straight and turn each of my feet out to the side, the first position," she recalled of that first lesson.[63]

In 1930, Carmen began training with Mrs. Sabin, who traveled from Tulsa, Oklahoma looking for new students. Soon Maria and Marjorie were giving recitals. Maria said she didn't care for Mrs. Sabin, calling her "a wretched instructor who never taught the basics."[64]

---

62. Tallchief, 1997.
63. Tallchief, 1997.
64. Tallchief, 1997.

Although her family was financially stable, Maria's mom was frugal. She didn't like having to buy new ballet shoes for Maria's growing feet. Ruth Tall Chief purchased shoes one size too big, then stuffed them with cloth pads. Maria was able to perform her routines but her shoes were uncomfortable. She wanted to please her mother. She was too young to realize it was okay to tell her mother the stuffed shoes hurt.

Maria had a brother, Jerry, who was born with rickets, a disease caused by Vitamin D deficiency. However, children treated with Vitamin D usually can live a normal life. When Jerry was four, he was kicked in the head by a horse, which caused learning disabilities. Specifically he had trouble reading. Maria's mom tried to teach him but when she was unsuccessful, she became frustrated. Maria believed her mother's frustration is what caused her to focus her attention on her daughters.

Maria began her formal education when she was five. She enrolled in Sacred Heart Catholic School. Maria was so bright she was immediately placed in a class two grades ahead of the other children her age. She was also shy. Maria loved being outdoors and enjoyed wandering around. She would often look for arrowheads in the grass and would ". . . shiver with excitement" when she found one.[65] She loved roaming the pastures. She also loved horses but after her brother's accident, she was forbidden from going near either.

Maria was a triple threat. She was smart. She was a skilled ballet dancer. She was musically gifted. She was a very good piano player. As a young girl, Maria's days were filled with school, ballet, and music lessons. "As a little girl, I didn't have much time to dream," she wrote in her autobiography, *Maria Tallchief: America's Prima Ballerina.*[66]

---

65. Tallchief, 1997.
66. Tallchief, 1997.

Maria and her sister performed routines created by Mrs. Sabin. They performed at community events like rodeos and fairs. Although both sisters were skilled dancers, they never competed. They were best friends according to Maria. Her mother dressed the two identically. Sometimes it was hard to tell them apart.

Maria's father never worked because of the oil royalties. But he liked to drink and this caused fighting between her parents. When the quarterly royalty checks arrived, he would go on drinking binges. The checks were for several thousand dollars. He received money from his real estate holdings but most of the family's money came from the royalty checks. Alexander Tall Chief would often disappear for an entire week during his drunken binges.

California dreaming

Ruth Tall Chief grew weary of life in Oklahoma. She convinced her husband to move to Los Angeles. He didn't object because he loved to play golf. The warm Los Angeles weather would allow him to play golf year-round. In 1933, the family headed to Los Angeles without really knowing where they would live.

A stop for gas settled the matter. While her husband fueled up, Ruth Tall Chief took the girls to get a hamburger and soda at the drugstore. She asked the druggist if he knew of any good dancing schools in the area. There was one right in the neighborhood: Ernest Belcher's.

Without another thought, Ruth told her husband they would find a place in that very neighborhood. Maria wrote: "That was it. An anonymous man in an unfamiliar town decided our fate with those few words."[67] The family settled in the Wilshire District in Los Angeles.

When Maria enrolled in public school, she was placed back in third grade. The school did this, not because she wasn't bright but because ". . . public school teachers seemed to understand that an eight-year-old had no business being in the fifth grade," Maria said.[68] She was placed in an advanced program, known as the "Opportunity Class," but she was still ahead of her classmates.

At Belcher's, the sisters took ballet, tap, acrobatics, and Spanish dancing. Maria enjoyed everything except tumbling. She worked herself into a frenzy until her mother said it was okay for her to stop taking the class.

Mr. Belcher told Maria's mother her daughters hadn't been taught the proper foundations of ballet. They were talented but he said they had been ". . . put on pointe way, *way* too early," he said.[69] He added that it was surprising they hadn't been injured. On pointe is when ballerina's stand on the tips of their toes. The sisters started their ballet lesson from the beginning. Unlike Mrs. Sabin, Mr. Belcher was an excellent ballet teacher and Maria was eager to learn from him.

The family moved from Wilshire to Beverly Hills. The public schools were better academically in Beverly Hills, said Ruth Tall Chief. Maria attended Beverly Vista School. Her initial experience wasn't pleasant. Kids made fun of her last name. They asked her if it was "Tall" or "Chief." Some made war whooping sounds when she passed. Others asked if her father collected human scalps. Eventually the kids stopped teasing Maria, but she decided to *smoosh* her last name into one word.

67. Tallchief, 1997.
68. Tallchief, 1997.
69. Tallchief, 1997.

Maria and Marjorie progressed at Belcher's. They had recitals and per-formed at local events. A Native American dance routine was added to their performance after a man recommended it to their mother. The girls didn't like the routine. Maria said it wasn't an authentic Native-Ameri-can dance. Females don't normally dance in tribal ceremonies, she said. The girls wore fringed buckskin outfits. They wore ballet shoes under their moccasins. They sported headbands adorned with features and wore bells on their legs. Maria was glad when they outgrew the outfits and didn't have to do the routine. "I was relieved when we put those bells away for good," she said.[70]

When Maria was 12 years old, her mother enrolled the sisters in a new ballet school. Another mother told her Bronislava Nijinska was opening a ballet studio. Nijinska was a famous Polish ballet dancer and choreogra-pher. Maria said she wasn't sure her mother knew who Nijinska was, but she plopped her kids from Belcher's without notifying him.

Because she had a limited English vocabulary, Nijinska often demonstrated ballet techniques. Students called her Madame and most were in awe of her magical footwork. Her husband Nicholas Singaevsky would sometimes translate for her but his English was also limited. Between his translations and Madame's demonstrations or firm taps on the shoulder, students gen-erally got the idea.

"Madame say you look like spaghetti," Singaevsky would say.[71]

"Madame say when you sleep, sleep like ballerina. Even on street wait-ing for bus, stand like ballerina."[72]

---

70. Tallchief, 1997.
71. Tallchief, 1997.
72. Tallchief, 1997.

A young Bronislava Nijinska poses for a photo in 1908.

It was during this time Maria decided she definitely wanted to become a ballerina. When Madame realized Maria was serious *and* talented, she began paying more attention to her. Maria said soon ". . . she was treating me like her protégée."[73]

When Maria was 15 years old, Madame presented three of her choreographed ballets. One of the ballets was *Chopin Concerto.* Maria was certain she would land one of the lead dance roles. The music Madame was using — Chopin's *Piano Concerto in E Minor* — was familiar to Maria. She was still taking piano lessons and was currently playing the concerto. One role went to a young dancer named Cyd Charisse. Charisse later became a famous movie star.

To Maria's surprise, she didn't get the second role. She was devastated. During rehearsals, Maria gave a lukewarm performance. Maria's mother told her: "You have to show that you want to dance with all your heart."[74] During the next rehearsal, Maria danced with renewed passion. She was rewarded with the second lead dancer role.

On the night of the performance, the sisters were running late. They didn't realize they needed to arrive two hours early for makeup and to warm up. During rehearsals, the floor was slippery and hard. For the performance, canvas cloths were laid out. Because of their late appearance, Maria and Marjorie didn't have time to rehearse on the covered floor.

Maria recalled her disappointing entrance: ". . . I stood in the wings waiting for my cue, and when I heard it, I made my entrance. As soon as I started dancing, I slipped. I recovered quickly and went on, but I was shaken," she said.[75]

---

73. Tallchief, 1997.
74. Tallchief, 1997.
75. Tallchief, 1997.

Maria was sure Madame would have something to say about the unfortunate flop. Surprisingly, Nijinska didn't say anything. Madame remained Maria's teacher throughout her high school years, although she would sometimes train with other teachers visiting the Los Angeles area.

Maria was college-bound — or so she thought. During Maria's senior year, her father made an announcement. He had paid for all of her dancing lessons and now it was time for her to get a job. The years between ages 17 and 20 are important in the life of a dancer. Maria said if she expected to become a professional ballerina, she needed to get started.

Her first audition was for an MGM movie, *Presenting Lily*. The musical starred Judy Garland, famous for playing Dorothy in the *Wizard of Oz*, in her first adult role. Maria was a dancing extra. After the experience, Maria knew she didn't want to dance in movies.

She was trying to figure out what she could do to earn money when her mother called. David Lichine, a dancer/teacher Maria studied with when he visited Los Angeles, and his wife Tatiana Riabouchinska, a Russian ballerina, had a proposition. During the summer, the couple was headed to New York to dance at Ballet Theatre. Riabouchinska said Maria could tag along. This would be an opportunity for Maria to audition for the famous Ballet Russe.

Professional ballerina

Shortly after arriving in New York, Maria went to the Ballet Russe office. She glided in and asked to audition for Mr. Denham. The secretary told her that Mr. Denham was busy. They didn't need dancers anyway, she said.

This photo was taken for the front cover of Dance Magazine in 1954.

Maria was heartbroken. But a few days later, she received a call from that same secretary. Maria didn't even recall leaving her contact information. They needed a dancer after all for a Canadian tour that was starting immediately. Mr. Denham remembered Maria so she didn't have to audition.

This was in 1942 and the company needed dancers because of World War II. Some of the Russian dancers had "Nansens" passports. These documents classified the dancers as *Displaced Persons* and prevented them from leaving the United States.

Luckily, there were two dancer spots available. The other spot went to an American girl named Gertrude Tyven, who used the last name Svobodina. Some dancers "Russianized" their names. This was the practice of making one's name sound Russian, the assumption being Russians were better ballet dancers.

The company soon boarded an overnight train to Montreal. During the tour, the routines varied nightly. Maria had to learn new routines quickly. "Dancing new roles on short notice was a way of life in the Ballet Russe . . . It didn't trouble me. I was not self-conscious. I was comfortable going out and showing what I could do, whatever the risks," she said.[76]

At the end of the tour, one of the dancers dropped out. This opened up a permanent spot for one lucky ballerina. The position went to Maria. Her payment was $40 weekly. That's the equivalent of about $605 in 2018.

On the first day of rehearsals, Maria was shocked when she walked in and heard music from *Chopin Concerto*. The she saw Madame Nijinska. The Ballet Russe was adding two of Madame's ballets to their repertoire. The regular chorographer had quit and Madame had stepped in temporarily.

It was during this time that 17-year-old Betty Marie changed her name. The company had added an American ballet, *Rodeo, or The Courting at Burnt Ranch*. Agnes de Mille wrote the ballet.

One night de Mille told the young dancer to change her name. "There are so many Bettys and Elizabeths in the ballet," she said.[77] She suggested she transform her middle name. She told Maria to change her last name to "Tallchieva." Maria was proud of her heritage and wouldn't budge on

76. Tallchief, 1997.
77. Tallchief, 1997.

the last name. However, she decided to use Maria as her first name. She officially became Maria Tallchief.

 Maria's parents continued to call her Betty or Betty Marie even after she changed her name.

Although Maria was making $40 a week, the ballet deducted money for the dancers hotel rooms when they traveled. The dancers used a trick called "ghosting." One person rented the room and three shared it. One slept on the mattress, another on the bed's box spring, while the third dozed on the floor.

The dancers also had to be frugal when paying for meals. Maria mainly ate a $.25 (about $3.78 in 2018) plate spaghetti meal from a restaurant on Broadway. She didn't eat much when the company was on the road either.

Maria's parents sent money tucked into letters — $5 here, $10 there. But she didn't want the other dancers to think she had more money than they. She saved the extra money, hiding it away in her suitcase. She ended up losing 15 pounds from not eating enough and working too hard. Despite the poverty, the hard work, and the weight loss, Maria loved being part of the ballet. The tour even made it to Los Angeles. Maria was excited to see her family *and* sleep in her own bed.

Balanchine

In 1944, the great Russian choreographer George Balanchine signed with Ballet Russe to choreograph dances for a show called *Song of Norway*. Maria became fascinated with him but was shy and awkward in his presence. The show received wonderful reviews after performances in Los Angeles and San Francisco.

The production wasn't part of the company's regular season. They were merely helping with the production, and it was soon time for the dancers to leave and prepare for their regular ballet season. The producer of the show offered Maria a spot but she declined. The position came with a raise but "I was a ballet dancer, not an actress or musical performer. [Her] place was with the Ballet Russe, not on Broadway."[78]

 Before the beginning of the next season Maria's mom stepped step in and re-negotiate her daughter's contract. Mr. Denham agreed to $50 ($700 in 2018) a week and he promoted Maria to soloist.

Balanchine also signed on to choreograph for Ballet Russe through the remainder of the season. *Ballet Imperial* was one of the programs Balanchine choreographed. One night before a performance in Chicago, Balanchine unexpectedly told Maria she was going to dance second lead during the premiere. Maria almost fainted. She was a good dancer but she didn't think she was ready to dance second lead in his production. Since Balanchine thought she was, Maria worked hard to learn the new routine.

Over the course of the next few months, the two grew closer. But they kept it professional. They talked always of dancing and nothing more, she said. Balanchine continued to give Maria roles and she worked hard to improve her ballet skills. She said: ". . . performing Balanchine's work taught me how to project. Dancing with confidence and authority in his ballets allowed me to show people exactly who I was and what I could do. The progress I made in one year was astonishing."[79]

Once Balanchine's contract with Mr. Denham ended, he planned to start his own company, Ballet Society. He'd had these plans before World War II

---

78. Tallchief, 1997.
79. Tallchief, 1997.

but put them on hold. His financial backer and business partner Lincoln Kirstein had served during the war.

Kirstein was a writer and patron of the arts. Now that he was home, plans for the ballet company could proceed. Balanchine's days with Ballet Russe were slowing ticking away. One night in Los Angeles after a performance, Balanchine asked Maria to meet with him.

"Maria, I want you to be my wife," he said without much preamble.[80]

Maria was so caught off guard she almost fell out of her seat. She wasn't sure she'd heard him correctly. He repeated his proposition: "Yes, I would like to marry you. I think it would be the most wonderful thing."[81]

Maria was stunned. They were friends, close friends, but nothing more (at least in her mind). She still called him Mr. Balanchine. He was also 20 years older than Maria. "I'm not sure that I love you. I feel that I hardly know you," she finally answered.[82]

Balanchine said he didn't care. "If it doesn't work out, well, that's fine too," he reasoned.[83]

She told him she would think about it. "I was barely a young woman. Marriage to Mr. Balanchine? Perhaps it would be the most wonderful thing," she thought to herself.[84]

---

80. Tallchief, 1997.
81. Tallchief, 1997.
82. Tallchief, 1997.
83. Tallchief, 1997.
84. Tallchief, 1997.

She wanted to talk with her parents but she thought she'd discuss the proposal with her friend Vida Brown first. She told Brown that "George" had proposed.

"*George, who?*" asked Brown.[85] When Maria said Balanchine, Brown almost choked on her sandwich. Then they both started laughing.

Brown asked Maria if she wanted to marry Balanchine. "*You know, I do*," she answered.[86]

Maria was starting to have feelings for Balanchine. He was ". . . everything a young girl could want - witty, debonair, handsome," she said.[87]

The age difference wasn't important. She shared his passion for music and ballet. "Why wouldn't I want to spend the rest of my life with him?" she said.[88]

Maria decided to accept Balanchine's proposal. She hurried home and told her parents. When she told her mother, ". . . she looked at me as if I were out of my mind," said Maria.[89]

She paced the floor, wringing her hands and shaking her head. Her objections were threefold:

1. He was divorced.

2. He was a *foreigner!*

3. He was twice Maria's age.

---

85. Tallchief, 1997.
86. Tallchief, 1997.
87. Tallchief, 1997.
88. Tallchief, 1997.
89. Tallchief, 1997.

She told Maria the whole idea was idiotic.

"What's wrong with you?" she screamed.[90] Maria's Aunt Pearl was visiting, and she thought the idea was wonderful. She knew all about Balanchine and thought he was a good catch. Maria's father didn't speak against Balanchine personally. He was against his daughter marrying anyone. He said she should focus on her ballet career.

When she talked to Balanchine about her parents' objections, he wasn't concerned. They would come around, he said. The couple returned to New York for rehearsals and continued to openly spend time together. He was romantic, taking Maria on horse-drawn carriage rides in Central Park. Soon she *was* falling in love with him.

The couple married on August 16, 1946. They were married at the Manhattan County Courthouse. Her parents didn't attend.

 George Balanchine's real name was Georgi Melitnovitch Balanchivadze.

Because they were both busy, their honeymoon was a country weekend getaway at a friend's house in Lee, Massachusetts. Maria's contract with Ballet Russe had six months left on it; she wasn't able to join her husband's new company until after it ended.

Balanchine had received an invitation from the Paris Opera to work in their company for six months. He'd received the invite before Ballet Society was on her feet. Once she was up and running he was able to leave for Paris. Maria's contract wasn't up until March 1947 but Balanchine needed to leave in February. His young bride would join him later.

---

90. Tallchief, 1997.

Near the end of their time in Paris, Maria's sister and her fiancé arrived. They were both involved in ballet and their troupe was performing in Vichy. They planned to marry while in France. At the ceremony was Madame Nijinska, who reportedly didn't like the groom. Maria said she was glad to see her old teacher but still felt intimidated by her. She also wondered what she thought of her marriage to Balanchine. She treated her warmly but they didn't get a chance to really talk because she and Balanchine had to head back to Paris for their return trip to New York.

Prima Ballerina

This is a headshot of Maria Tallchief from April 1961.

Maria's time in Paris elevated her skills as a ballerina, but she knew she could do so much more under Balanchine's guidance. "I was eager to put myself in his hands, enthusiastic about becoming exactly what he wanted me to be . . ." Maria said.[91]

---

91. Tallchief, 1997.

The Ballet Society was renting space from the City Center of Music. One night Martin Baum, chairman of the center's executive committee, approached Balanchine and Kirstein. He wanted the Ballet Society to become the center's resident dance troupe. They would have to change their name to the New York City Ballet, but they could continue their season performances. They would also provide ballets for the New York City Opera. It was good news because they would now have a permanent home.

They enthusiastically agreed to the arrangement, making an announcement to the troupe a few days later. But the newly named company had problems. According to Maria, "Seasons were brief, money was tight, and our deficits showed no sign of diminishing."[92]

The first season opened on October 11, 1948 with three dances choreographed by Balanchine. The short season had only 14 performances. They danced on Monday and Tuesdays only. The opera performed the remainder of the week. The company was getting attention but attendance wasn't as high as expected. At the end of the first season, Mr. Baum decided to allow the company a separate season to help boost attendance. The season ran for two consecutive weeks in January, with 10 performances, Thursday through Sunday.

Balanchine didn't take a salary but he still had to support himself and his young wife. He took paid choreography gigs during the off-season.

 **FAST FACT** Maria's parents eventually warmed up to the marriage, especially her mother who was charmed by Balanchine.

---

92. Tallchief, 1997.

The company continued to have an abbreviated season. Balanchine worried he might lose some of his best dancers. Maria was also worried. She was only performing 30 times a year. At 23, that amount of performances wasn't enough for her.

Maria was able to get work with the Ballet Theatre, but it was short-lived, performing from the winter of 1949 to June of that same year.

The New York City Ballet didn't perform during the summer of 1949. With four months off, the couple decided to drive cross-country in Balanchine's new Mercury convertible. At the end of the summer, they returned to New York and began rehearsing daily and preparing for the upcoming season.

In July, the company embarked on a five-week English tour, beginning in London. Maria was the leading ballerina and she was always conscientious of how much her performance reflected on the company. She knew as Balanchine's wife she also had a special role to play. She remarked that ". . . some days the responsibility weighed heavily on me."[93] "That my private life and my job were one and the same often made me feel that I was always working," she added.[94]

She wasn't unhappy but she wanted to slow down. She wanted to meet people her age and people who weren't dancers. She was also thinking about starting a family.

But her husband didn't want Maria to have children. He liked kids but felt Maria's career was more important. "His attitude was that anyone could have babies. Only a few people were able to dance," Maria said.[95]

---

93. Tallchief, 1997.
94. Tallchief, 1997.
95. Tallchief, 1997.

Balanchine was staking the success of his company on Maria's performances. So taking time off to have a baby wasn't feasible. "We were in complete agreement on that . . . yet something in me was stirring," she said.[96]

Then a curious thing happened. While at a friend's party in New York, Maria met a young pilot named Elmourza Natirboff. There was instant attraction. He was in his mid-twenties, ". . . dark and romantic-looking."[97]

The next day he called and invited Maria to the races at Belmont. She had always wanted to go but Balanchine never seemed to have the time or desire to go. Maria asked him if it was okay if she went with Natirboff. Balanchine told her to ahead.

Maria had second thoughts. She was attracted to Elmourza, and she was sure the feelings were mutual. She decided to go anyway. The date was completely innocent. However, the next day Elmourza started calling Maria often.

She liked the attention. Soon Maria wondered if she was falling in love with the young man. Before she left on the London tour, Elmourza surprised Maria. He told her to divorce Balanchine and marry him.

Maria said, "I was shocked and confused and didn't know what to say. What upset me most was deep down I *wanted* to have a romance with Elmourza. But how could that be possible? Leaving George for another man was unthinkable."[98]

Maria went to her husband and told him about her mixed feelings for Elmourza. Balanchine said he didn't want to separate. He wanted to know

96. Tallchief, 1997.
97. Tallchief, 1997.
98. Tallchief, 1997.

what she wanted. She told him she didn't know. But her husband didn't seemed upset by the news. She noticed he seemed eager to see her happy ". . . almost too eager."[99]

Then he told her that if they divorced, nothing would change. She would still be his star ballerina. With the matter settled, she decided they should divorce. "The entire episode was painless, rather matter-of-fact," she said. "I was amazed."[100]

Balanchine only asked that they wait until after the tour to make an official announcement. When they returned to New York, they made the announcement and Maria moved in with Vida. She began openly dating Elmourza but wasn't in a hurry to get married again.

Maria's suspicions that Balanchine was too eager to end the marriage were true. He had fallen in love with a young dancer, Tanaquil (Tanny) Le Clercq. She was just four years younger than Maria. Balanchine and Tanny married shortly after the divorce was final.

 Over her career, Maria danced in many ballets. Some of her most memorable roles were in *Orpheus, Scotch Symphony, Miss Julie, Firebird,* and *The Nutcracker.*

Work resumed and Balanchine continued to create stunning ballets, many with Maria as the centerpiece. She was his muse, he said. Maria was an audience favorite by the time she was 26 years old. Many magazine and newspapers wrote glowing reviews about her.

---

99. Tallchief, 1997.
100. Tallchief, 1997.

Maria Tallchief and Nicholas Magallanes perform in The Nutcracker in 1954.

In her private life, Maria continued her romance with Elmourza. But they both had busy schedules. He was working for a private airplane charter company and his boss kept him in the air a lot. It was understood they would marry after Maria's divorce was final.

By 1952, the New York City Ballet was working longer seasons and touring often. They had their second European tour, which ran for five months beginning in April. They visited France, Spain, Italy, England, the Netherlands, Scotland, and Germany.

Maria was excited about the French leg of the tour. She wanted to visit Marjorie, who was living in Paris. Marjorie was still with the ballet. She was also pregnant with twins. She gave birth to adorable baby boys after Maria had moved on to perform in Holland. They named the boys Alexander and George.

Endings and New Beginnings

After returning to New York, Maria's divorce was finalized. "But no tears were shed, at least not then. It took awhile for me to absorb the impact," she recalled.[101]

And true to his word, Maria's professional role didn't change. "Quite the opposite," Maria said. "With every year, he seemed to see more and more in my work."[102]

On October 4, 1952, Maria and Elmourza married. The couple moved into a tiny one-room apartment on New York's East Side. It was all they could afford. Although she was working hard, Maria was only making about $100 (about $930 in 2018) a week and her new husband was earning about the same amount. There wasn't much money to divide during the divorce settlement so she'd walked away with nothing, much to her mother's disappointment.

Maria said she liked Elmourza and was physically attracted to him. She said she had probably been in love with him at one time. "But from day one I understood our marriage was a mistake. Still, I tried to make it work, but I was fighting the odds," she said.[103]

---

101. Tallchief, 1997.
102. Tallchief, 1997.
103. Tallchief, 1997.

 In 1953, the Washington Press Club awarded a Woman of the Year plaque to Maria. She was designated a "Woman of Achievement".

Maria's status as a prima ballerina continued to grow. She was even asked to perform during President Dwight Eisenhower's inaugural ceremonies. The president came backstage to meet her and tell her how much he admired her.

Rudolf Orthwine presents Maria Tallchief with a Dance Magazine award in April 1961.

At home, Maria's home life was crumbling. She was married to man she didn't love. He ". . . didn't understand what it meant to be married to a ballerina," she said.[104]

---

104. Tallchief, 1997.

Tribal honor

In 1953, the Osage tribe and the state of Oklahoma designated June 29 as Maria Tallchief Day. The tribe gave her a new title: Princess Wa-Xthe-Thonba (Princess Two Standards). The name, chosen by her grandmother, was a reminder that although she was a successful prima ballerina, "... she was still her grandchild, an Osage woman, and a daughter of the tribe."[105]

During the summer of 1953, the company performed in Los Angeles for a month, then embarked on another European tour. It lasted the entire fall season and included stops in Italy, France, Belgium, Denmark, Germany, and Switzerland.

After returning home, Maria's marital situation wasn't improving. Finally, she left Elmourza, flying to Mexico for a quick divorce.

After the tour, Maria received some more exciting news. The Ballet Russe, which had been inactive for a few seasons, was planning a revival. Columbia Arts Management agreed to back the tour for Mr. Denham but the director, Frederick Schang, had one condition: Maria had to dance with the troupe. For her role, they agreed to pay her $2,000 a week (that's the equivalent of about $18,477 in 2018).

"If you accept, you'll be making the highest salary ever given to a ballerina in the history of dance," he said.[106]

They understood Maria was committed to Balanchine. They offered her a temporary position. They hoped her name would draw people in and help revived the troupe.

---

105. Tallchief, 1997.
106. Tallchief, 1997.

Maria Tallchief and Erik Bruhn pose together on the cover of
Dance Magazine June 1961.

After thinking the offer over and talking to Balanchine, Maria accepted the
offer. The contract included over 179 dates in 103 cities over the next year.
Maria's return to Ballet Russe was picked up by major publications. She
received high praise. In an article in *Newsweek*, she was called ". . . the fin-
est American-born ballerina the twentieth century had ever produced."[107]

Her technique was so graceful, the dance critic for the New York Times,
John Martin, said: "You find yourself thinking of her secondarily as a
dancer and primarily as an artist."[108]

---

107. Tallchief, 1997.
108. Tallchief, 1997.

When her time with Ballet Russe ended, Maria flew to France to catch up with her troupe. They were on yet another European tour. Maria resumed her role as primary dancer.

After returning to the United States, the company had a full schedule of performances. Maria also moved a new apartment and for the first time was living alone. She felt isolated but didn't have much time to think about it because she was rehearsing, traveling, and performing most of the time.

While working in Chicago, Maria made a new friend, Dorothy Goettsch, whose aunt was a ballet teacher. One day Goettsch invited Maria to go sailing with her and a few friends. Maria was excited because she'd never sailed before.

During the excursion, Maria met a young man sailor named Henry Paschen, called "Buzz."

Maria thought he was attractive. She also thought he might be Dorothy's boyfriend. There was another man who Dorothy seemed googly-eyed over, but Maria noticed Buzz was paying a lot of attention to Dorothy. Then again, he paid lots of attention to Maria.

Buzz said he'd never met any dancers before or attended the ballet. Maria invited him to a performance. A few nights later, he attended a show at the Opera House.

After that night, they saw each other daily during Maria's time in Chicago. Maria was attracted to Buzz but she wasn't serious about him. She didn't plan on seeing him once the troupe moved on. He was two years younger and didn't ". . . have his feet on the ground," she said.[109]

---

109. Tallchief, 1997.

Besides, Maria had recently started dating a Texas multi-millionaire. He was older than Balanchine and her father didn't care for him, but Maria did. She said she wasn't in love with him, but she wanted to see where the relationship might lead. He was married but living separately from his wife.

When she left for New York, Maria didn't expect to see Buzz again. A few weeks later, he arrived in New York. Maria was happy to see him, but her Texas beau wasn't. Buzz was just a friend, she told him. Maria didn't like her new boyfriend's behavior. He was jealous, possessive, and sometimes threw tantrums. But she wasn't ready to let him go just yet. She was starting to have feelings for Buzz, too.

One night when Maria arrived home with her Texas boo, a package was waiting for her from Chicago. When she opened it, she found a negligee and a note from Buzz. Old Tex threw a fit. Maria tried to laugh it off. She assured him that her relationship with Buzz was platonic. But he didn't buy it.

"I was tired of arguing," Maria said.[110] "Besides, his demand that I see only him was draining me of energy and good humor," she added.[111]

He continued to profess his love for Maria. He swore he wanted to marry her. Yet, neither Old Tex nor his estranged wife would file for divorce. After Old Tex stormed out, Maria called Buzz and yelled at him for causing trouble. Unfazed, he told her he was planning a trip soon to New York.

"How can you be sure I'll even see you?" she asked.[112] But she said she knew in her heart she would.

---

110. Tallchief, 1997.
111. Tallchief, 1997.
112. Tallchief, 1997.

Meanwhile, Maria continued seeing Tex, although she was annoyed with his possessive behavior. Maria relationship with Buzz was getting stronger. Finally, on New Year's Eve 1955, Tex ordered Maria to never see Buzz again. They argued for a while and then he left. Maria tried to rest because she had a live television performance in a few hours. When she returned home, she decided to end her toxic relationship with the Texan.

Maria was already spending more time with Buzz and soon she decided to take him home to meet her parents. Her mother wasn't too impressed, mainly because of his occupation. He told her he was a bricklayer. But Maria said he was toying with her mother, ". . . making her think he was a laborer."[113]

Buzz had started out as a bricklayer at his father's construction company. Now he was actually an executive at the company, Paschen Contractors. "He calculated what it would cost to build a particular project so the company could bid on it competitively," Marie explained in her memoirs.[114] His family was prosperous, and Buzz grew up in a large house complete with servants but he wasn't pretentious or snotty.

Maria's dad, however, liked the young man and they became friends. Maria had also met Buzz's parents, and they seemed pleased with their son's new girlfriend.

On June 3, 1956, Maria married for the third time. The ceremony took place in Chicago with Buzz's cousin, a circuit court judge, officiating. Buzz had been married before and had a daughter. He was very close to her and that pleased Maria because she wanted kids but none of her previous husbands had.

---

113. Tallchief, 1997.
114. Tallchief, 1997.

The young couple rushed into the marriage so quickly they didn't stop to think about important issues like where they would live. Buzz's family business was in Chicago, and Maria's life was in New York.

For the third time, Maria didn't have a proper honeymoon. She had to fly to Los Angeles the next day. The newlyweds decided to postpone their honeymoon until the fall. The ballet was going on another trip to Europe and Buzz was tagging along for part of the tour.

Before Maria left for Europe, she thought she might be pregnant. In those days, they didn't have instant at-home pregnancy test. It also took a few days to get the results from the doctor. Maria saw a doctor but she was leaving the next day. He said he would send the results to her.

A few days later Betty Cage, an administrator with the ballet, pulled Maria to the side.

"You're pregnant!" she said.[115]
"I'm what!" Maria screamed.
"You're expecting."
"How do you know?"
"I got a note from your doctor."

She handed Maria the letter, which confirmed she was pregnant. Maria Tallchief, prima ballerina was expecting her first child at the age of 31. Buzz was overjoyed. He loved being a father but Maria also suspected he thought becoming a mother would make her settle down in Chicago.

---

115. Tallchief, 1997

Maria was feeling fine physically. Then one day she started feeling unwell when the troupe was in Zurich. She went to a doctor and he told her she might miscarry. He recommended complete bed rest.

Maria was concerned for her baby, of course, but she was also concerned about not being able to dance. She contacted Balanchine and told him the doctor's recommendations. He assured her it was okay if she couldn't perform. The health of her baby was more important.

In a few days, the troupe left for Venice but Maria was still not feeling well. She remained behind. She would either catch up on the next stop (in France) or head home. Maria was feeling down and decided to call her sister. Marjorie suggested Maria come to Paris and rest at her house. After consulting with the doctors, Maria got the okay to travel by train to her sister's house.

In Paris, she consulted another doctor who recommended the same plan of treatment: complete bed rest. Despite following the doctors' order, Maria's symptoms didn't improve. Unfortunately, she lost the baby.

Instead of returning to the troupe after her miscarriage, Maria went to Chicago. Her sister and brother-in-law had performances in the city and this seemed like a good place to recuperate after her devastating loss. Maria was despondent for a while but eventually was able to pull herself together. She was ready to return to work when the 1956 winter season began.

There was another issue still left unsettled: where would the young couple live? Maria assumed Buzz would move to New York. The Big Apple was the center of her career. He, on the other hand, assumed she would move to Chicago. The family business was booming and he was inching his way up the ladder to become president. He felt it was time for Maria to consider retiring since she was over 30 years old.

Then tragedy struck the ballet world; Tanny contracted polio during the European tour.

When Balanchine and Tanny returned to the United States, he devoted much of his time to his bride's recovery. Lincoln Kirstein and Betty Cage took over much of the responsibility of the troupe.

The following year, in the fall of 1957, Balanchine finally returned to the company. Maria described his return: "What I believed George wanted more than anything else was to return to work, and after the interval of enforced inactivity, creativity burst out of him in a torrent."[116]

He choreographed four new ballets and planned a revival of an old one. In 1958, the company began a six-month tour of the Far East including stops in Japan, Australia, and the Philippines. Lincoln would be in charge during the tour because Balanchine refused to leave Tanny alone for such a long time. Maria felt the same way about her new husband. Married less than a year, she didn't want to leave him for six months. Lincoln told her if she made the Japan dates, she could miss the rest of the tour.

In April 1958 after returning from Japan, Maria thought she might be pregnant again. In June, her doctor confirmed she was. Because of her previous miscarriage, Maria was urged to stop dancing immediately.

The couple rented a house for the summer in Winnetka, near Chicago. Maria had a barre installed in the basement so she could practice but again, she made sure not to over exert herself.

The pregnancy proceeded with any complications. In January 1959, daughter Elise Paschen was born.

---

116. Tallchief, 1997.

Elise Paschen
Elise didn't follow in her mother's footsteps, but she is an artist. Paschen is a widely published poet. She co-founded *Poetry in Motion*, a national program that places poetry posters in subway cars and buses.

When Elise was a few weeks old, Maria began practicing for return to the stage. A few weeks later, she flew to New York to rehearse for a live television performance.

At rehearsal Maria was a little stiff but soon she was back to normal. The live show was a success. "Motherhood had produced a glow in me and even though we were dancing on a concrete floor, I don't think I ever danced the role as well," she said.[117]

After her comeback show, she began regularly performing and was soon back in shape. In August, she flew with seven-month-old Elise to New York to join her troupe. She hired a Swiss nanny, Soeur Ruth, to help take care of Elise.

Shortly after she returned to work, Maria received a frantic call from her mother. Maria's dad was sick. She immediately flew to Oklahoma with Buzz, baby Elise, and Soeur Ruth. Maria's dad seemed in good spirits, but it was evident by his appearance that his health was shaky. Maria spoke with his doctor. Her father had a viral infection. They didn't know the cause but was treating him with antibiotics.

Maria wasn't able to stay long because she had commitments. Her father understood and encouraged her to go. A few days later, her mother called again to say Alexander Tall Chief was in a Tulsa hospital.

117. Tallchief, 1997.

Balanchine convinced Maria to fly her dad to a specialist in Chicago but they offered the same diagnosis: granuloma, a large mass of tissue caused by an infection. He remained in the hospital growing weaker by the day. Then he improved enough that he was discharged and sent back to Oklahoma. But before doctors could release him, Maria's father had a stroke. When it was obvious he wouldn't recover, they took him home to Oklahoma. In October 1959, he died.

Grief stricken, Maria returned to the New York City Ballet after a year's hiatus. But the tragic passing of her beloved father marred what should have been an exciting time. Tragedy would strike again when Maria received another frantic call — this time from Buzz. His father was in the hospital. He'd had a heart attack. By the time Maria arrived in Chicago from New York, Mr. Paschen was dead.

Life soon returned to normal for Maria, including a short stint with the Ballet Theatre. Initially, Maria was reluctant to sign a contract because it meant being away from her young daughter for six months. But she decided to join the tour, leaving Elise in the capable hands of Soeur Ruth.

After she returned, she decided to temporarily separate from Buzz. They still hadn't decided on where they would live. With his father passing, he definitely couldn't leave Chicago. Her life still centered on New York. She decided she needed to get away and have some time to think- time away from Buzz.

She packed up and made a surprise visit to Paris. But the surprise was her sister and brother-in-law were also packing. They had an engagement in South America, so they wouldn't be able to spend time with Maria.

After a brief respite, Maria made her way back to New York to rehearse for the upcoming season. Maria decided to remain in New York. Elise was old enough to start school and she needed a stable home base. Buzz remained in Chicago. Maria said although they were now estranged, they were on good terms. But he had already found a new romantic interest.

In addition to dancing, Maria taught ballet classes. In 1963, Maria was approached by ballerina Margot Fonteyn. She wanted to know if Maria was interested in teaching ballet to Jackie Kennedy's, (wife of President John F. Kennedy) daughter Caroline. The class would also include a few of Caroline's cousins.

Maria jumped at the chance. She would include Elise and a few of her classmates too. Balanchine agreed to let the girls perform on a small studio at his school. They would practice at Elise's school gym.

 Maria's students included Kate Burton, daughter of actor Richard Burton. Burton grew up to become an accomplished actress. You may know her as Sally Langston from ABC's *Scandal*. She also played Dr. Ellis Grey on *Grey's Anatomy*. And if you're a *Grimm* fan like the author, she played Nick's Aunt Marie.

Maria continued teaching and performing, but she was growing weary of traveling. And her daughter was growing up and she wanted Elise to have a steady homelife. She realized she still loved Buzz. "Buzz and I both understood we had this beautiful, intelligent, sensitive child, and we owed her a great responsibility. We decided to try to live together again . . ." she said.[118]

They saved their marriage and remained together until Buzz's death in 2004.

---

118. Tallchief, 1997.

Maria started seriously thinking about retiring. She was 41, still young enough to enjoy a quiet life with her family, but the lure of the stage kept drawing her back. She eventually decided to hang up her ballet slippers, retiring in 1966. She moved to Chicago and settled into her new role as wife and mother.

After retirement, ballet was still a part of Maria's life. She taught ballet and served as the artistic director of the Chicago Lyric Opera Ballet. She later founded the Chicago City Ballet, where she served as artistic director.

In December 2012, Maria broke her hip. On April 11, 2013, Maria died in Chicago. Her death was a result of this injury. She was 88 years old.

Throughout her life, Maria received numerous accolades. In 1996, Maria received the prestigious Kennedy Center Honors for her contributions to the arts. She was also inducted into the National Women's Hall of Fame. Three years later, she received the National Medal of Arts, another distinguished award given to individuals for their contributions to the arts.

Maria once said, "Above all, I wanted to be appreciated as a prima ballerina who happened to be a Native American, never as someone who was an American Indian ballerina."[119] However, that title is part of her legacy. But the distinction does not diminish her skills as a dancer. As America's first prima ballerina, Maria Tallchief set the standard for many young dancers who followed in her footsteps. Maria Tallchief took the ballet world by storm. Before Maria, the most revered ballet dancers were usually Russian. The idea of an American Indian dancer was unheard of. Maria proved it was possible for Native Americans to achieve success in the arts outside of traditional native dance rituals. Maria's success remains an inspiration to aspiring young dancers of all ethnicities.

---

119. Tallchief, 1997.

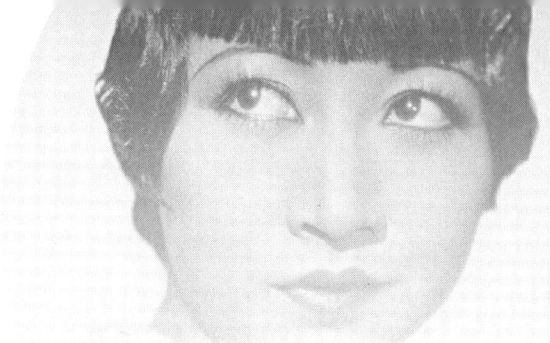

Chapter Seven

Anna May Wong

Hollywood Legend

Second Daughter

Anna May Wong was born January 3, 1905, in Los Angeles, California. She was a third-generation Chinese-American. Her birth name, Wong Liu Tsong, translates as:

Wong	**Liu**	**Tsong**
(the families surname)		
↓	↓	↓
yellow	*butterfly*	*second daughter*

Anna May's parents, Wong Sam Sing and Lee Gon Toy, owned Sam Kee Laundry on an integrated street near Chinatown. The family residence was on top of the laundry mat.

Laundry facilities

In the early 1900s, many people didn't have running water and washing machines wouldn't even be invented until 1908 (and were incredibly expensive for decades). Because of this, a lot of people chose to outsource their laundry where customers would drop their clothing off to be washed, dried, and ironed.

Anna May had six siblings:

- Wong Lew Ying (Lulu)

- Wong Yah Wing (James)

- Wong Way Ying (Frank)

- Wong Lew Choon (Marietta; died in infancy)

- Wong Lew Huang (Mary)

- Wong Kim Ying (Richard)

- Wong Suey Ying (Roger)

The Wong children worked in the laundry. Wong Sam Sing was described as a "controlling, traditional father" who expected his daughters to "obey without question and remain close to home."[120]

Anna May's and Lulu's education began at the California Street School. They tried to blend in but encountered racism. "Western children did not hesitate to use slurs against the young girls, pulling their hair and shoving them off the sidewalk," wrote Graham Russell Hodges, in *Anna May Wong: From Laundryman's Daughter to Hollywood Legend (2004)*.[121]

---

120. Hodges, 2004.
121. Hodges, 2004.

One bully jabbed Anna May with pins to see if Chinese children felt pain the same as others. Anna May wore more coats, and the bully brought longer pins. At one point, Anna May wore six coats for protection.

Her parents transferred the sisters to a safer school. At the Presbyterian Chinese Mission School in Chinatown, the teachers were white but the students were Chinese. The curriculum included core subjects like history, math, and English. The girls attended a Chinese-language school in the afternoons and on Saturdays. Anna May continued her education at Custer Street Junior High School and Lincoln High School.

This is a portrait of Anna May Wong circa 1935.

Anna May used a tip from a customer to see her first movie. She was mesmerized. Anna May began cutting class to watch matinees, using her lunch money to buy tickets. Eventually her father discovered Anna May's truancy. He whipped her with a bamboo stick, but she continued to dream of stardom. She practiced movie scenes in her bedroom. When companies began filming in Chinatown, Anna May's hung around the set. She dreamed of being "discovered."

Anna May began her acting career in silent films. Her first role was in 1919, when she was 14 years old. She was an extra in *The Red Lantern*. Anna May didn't receive film credit, but she was officially an actress. She ditched her college plans and ended her education after two years of high school to work as a full-time actress.

Her parent's disapproval caused friction, which led to physical and emotional stress for Anna May. Anna May's father tried to force her into an arranged marriage, but she refused.

Anna May had several small, uncredited roles after *The Red Lantern*. In 1920, she got a break when she was cast as "servant" in *Dinty*. In previous roles, she was a background actress — one indistinguishable face in a sea of thousands of Chinese extras. In *Dinty*, she was the only Asian actress in the scene.

The four-part Chinese chronicle, *Bits of Life* (1921*)*, was Anna May's first major role. She starred opposite legendary actor Lon Chaney. As Anna May's supporting role status increased, so did her paycheck. She made about $150.00 a week (about $1,480.00 in 2018) filming *Bits of Life*. Anna May began receiving kind reviews in the United States and abroad.

She was still living with her family and working in the laundry when not filming. She also gave some of the money she earned to her family. As her popularity soared, reporters dropped by unannounced. Her father was annoyed. He wanted his daughter to get married, but she rejected her father's wishes again. She didn't want a man to control her. Her parents didn't think she could make it as an actress in a society that didn't value Chinese people.

She also thought finding a husband might be difficult. "She knew that Chinese American men preferred Chinese-born women, who they felt were less spoiled than their American-born counterparts," wrote Hodges.[122] Anna May never married, possibly because of her feelings of independence.

The Thief of Bagdad (1924) was Anna May's breakout role. The movie stared Douglass Fairbanks, a superstar Hollywood actor. The movie was a success. Anna May's part was small, but memorable. She played the role of a slave to the princess, who was lead female role. Her character became a spy who ultimately betrayed her mistress.

After the movie's premiere, critics praised Anna May. She was featured in a two-page spread in *Picture Show* magazine. She was on the front cover of *Mon Ciné*, a popular French magazine.

Roles continued to pour in for the rising young star. She had small roles in *The 40th Door* and *The Alaskan* (both in 1924). Anna May's next role was in the critically acclaimed Paramount Picture movie *Peter Pan*. She received fourth billing as "Tiger Lily."

Can you believe Anna May's father *still* hounded her to get married? Fed up with his nagging, she bounced. But solo life was lonely. Her father proposed a solution: he offered to build a small apartment behind the laundry for Anna May. She could have freedom while not being totally alone.

---

122. Hodges, 2004.

This is a promotion poster for the 1924 *Peter Pan*
that Anna May played Tiger Lily in.

Anna May's next role in the *Forty Winks* (1924), was her biggest to date.
Critics called her performance "convincing," "outstanding," and "excellent."

She worked steadily, grabbing small roles. Some were flops, but she usually
received good reviews. After *Forty Winks,* she appeared in *His Supreme Moment,* followed by four movies in 1926: *Fifth Avenue, A Trip to Chinatown,
Silk Bouquet,* and *Desert's Toll.* Hodges wrote that none of the movies were
". . . of great consequence."[123]

---

123. Hodges, 2004.

With eight years of movie credits, 22-year-old Anna May Wong still struggled to land major roles — or major checks. In 1927, she had a part in *The Honorable Mr. Buggs*. She earned $667.00 (about $9,455.00 in 2018). In comparison, Pricilla Dean, the movie's star, earned $3,000.00 (about $42,500.00 in 2018). However, she earned more than the Japanese actor, Kimayama Sojin, who received a paltry $92.00 (about $1,300.00 in 2018).

What was stalling Anna May's career? A ban against interracial on-screen kissing was probably the culprit. Hollywood couldn't cast her in any role that called for kissing the lead actor. She was relegated to less desirable roles like prostitutes or drug dealers.

Despite these setbacks, Anna May was popular. She was stunningly beautiful. She graced the pages of popular magazines. She had a great sense of fashion.

Anna May became fed up with Hollywood. She thought she might have better luck in Germany. Her family was understandably concerned about their young daughter leaving the country, so she agreed to take Lulu with her. The sisters left the United States in March 1928.

Anna May was considered a major movie star by German filmmakers, so she immediately found work. She started filming the movie, *Song* in May. When she wasn't working, she explored Berlin. She attended the opera and theater. She hung out with Berlin's artistic community. She attended parties thrown by German aristocrats. Anna May made an impression on the Germans, who had limited contact with Chinese people.

When she finished filming, Anna May visited Paris, and then headed to London to film *Piccadilly*. "Her impact on the public was immediate," wrote Hodges. "People mobbed her everywhere she went, making her forays into the city difficult."[124]

Young girls tried to look like her. They painted their faces to mimic her skin tone. They cut their hair in the same style. They imitated her clothing choices. If social media existed during her time, she would have had a *huge* following.

In July, Lulu returned to America. Anna May returned to Berlin at the end of the summer for the premiere of *Song*. Most critics praised her performance.

In February 1929, Anna May returned to London for the opening of *Piccadilly*. Reviews were mixed but mostly favorable. During this time, Anna May made her entrance into the theater world. She appeared in a production called *Circle of Chalk*.

The transition from silent to talking movies was in full swing. Unfortunately, some critics didn't like Anna May's voice. A critic in *Sketch Magazine* wrote: ". . . to behold her is a pleasure, to hear her just a little strain."[125]

Anna May had a busy film schedule. In October 1929, she was off to England to film *Elstree Calling*. She then completed three films: *Road to Dishonour*, *Hai-Tang*, and *L'Amour des Choses*.

In Europe, she crisscrossed from Berlin, to Paris, to London. She took another stab at theater, appearing in the London production *On the Spot*. Her next performance was a Viennese opera, *Die Chinesiche Tanzerin* (The Chinese Dancer) in August 1930. The opera was scheduled to run through the

---

124. Hodges, 2004.
125. Hodges, 2004.

end of October. The show ended in September because of critical reviews. Anna May decided it was time to return to America. In October 1930, she waved goodbye to Europe.

25-year-old Anna May Wong got her first return role before she set foot on U.S. soil. She was cast in the Broadway production of *On the Spot*.

On the Spot opened on Broadway in the fall of 1930. Anna May's return to the United States was ruined by a family tragedy. Her mother was hit and killed in November while crossing the street at only 43 years old.

 There are two versions of what happened after her mother's death. In one, Anna May refused to leave New York because she was performing. In the second version, Wong Sam Sing kept his wife's body in a mausoleum until his daughter returned to Los Angeles in June 1931.

When she returned to California, Anna May worked with her former studio, Paramount Pictures. She played a character in *Daughter of the Dragon* (1931*)*. This was the first movie featuring two Asian stars. The other lead was actor Sessue Hayakawa. Anna May's salary increased when she returned home. But she was still underpaid in relation to her co-stars.

Let's take a closer look:

- **Anna May** earned **$6,000** for four weeks of filming (about $97,369.00 in 2018)

- **Hayakawa** earned **$10,000** (about $162,282.00 in 2018)

- **Warner Oland** (the white, top-billed star) earned **$12,000** (about $194,740.00 in 2018).

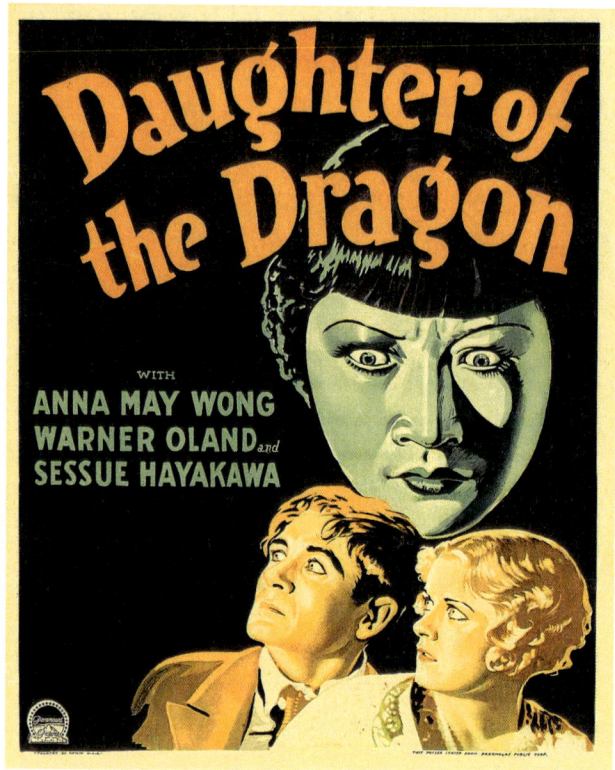

This is a film poster for *Daughter of the Dragon*.

Anna May did earn enough to help her siblings. She paid for all of their college education.

The film received positive reviews. Critics mostly praised both Anna May's acting and voice. After filming, Anna May returned to her role in *On the Spot*. She performed in Los Angeles and across the country.

In the fall of 1931, a great opportunity came her way. She was offered third billing in *Shanghai Express* (1932). "Had there been such an award then, the consensus is that Anna May would have received as Oscar for her supporting role," wrote Hodges.[126]

126. Hodges, 2004.

Anna May was successful in Europe and the United States before she was 27 years old. She landed roles in several foreign movies in the 1930s including *Tiger Bay (1933),* and *Chu Chin Chow (1934).* She returned to Hollywood in 1934, cast in Paramount's *Limehouse Blues.*

That year, Anna May's father moved to China. His business was gone. In its place was the newly constructed railway terminal, Union Station. After she finished filming, Anna May returned to Europe before returning to America in June 1935.

When she didn't get the lead part in a movie she wanted, Anna May decided to visit China. Most of her family had relocated there. She planned to stay in China for a year, learning the language and culture.

She arrived February 9, 1936. A cameraman with the Hearst Corporation documented Anna May's journey. Fans and reporters lined the dock waiting for arrival by boat. During her first days in China, Anna May gave interviews and rubbed elbows with the elite. Some Chinese citizens and the press criticized her behavior. They said she was acting like a typical rich tourist. She ate in expensive restaurants and slept in a fancy hotel. She wasn't interested in spending time with locals or learning about the Chinese culture, they said. They even criticized her marital status.

But she was unfazed. On her last day in China, she told a reporter the visit had been a success and that she hoped to return annually. She left for the United States on October 23, arriving in San Francisco on November 28. In California, Anna May resumed filming. She was cast in the MGM movie *Hollywood Party,* released in 1937. This vehicle starred the famous actor, Clark Gable.

Anna May Wong poses for a photo in 1935.

She appeared in a few theater productions and completed a film for Paramount, *Daughter of Shanghai* (1938) As the top-billed star, Anna May received $4,166.67 (about $71,374.19 in 2018). How did this compare to her co-stars? Philip Ahn received a paltry $1,000.00 or about $17,130 in 2018. But Anna May was still making less than white actors.

For Anna May's next movie, *Dangerous to Know* (1938*)* she was listed as a "featured player." Let's check out the pay gap between the stars.

- **Anna May** earned **$5,000.00** (about $85, 650.00 in 2018)

- **Gail Patrick** (a featured actor) earned **$14, 437.00** (about $247, 300.00 in 2018)

Despite her impressive acting career, Hollywood refused to pay Anna May a comparable salary to white actors. Even when cast in similar roles (as featured actors, for example), she earned a third of what her white counterparts made.

Her next role was in *When Were You Born?* (1938), a Warner Brothers production but Paramount loaned Anna May to the studio (she was still under contract). This was followed by *King of Chinatown* (1939). Anna May received a salary bump because Paramount was happy with earnings from her previous movie. She earned $9,790.00 (about $167,700.00 in 2018). Her last movie for Paramount was *Island of Lost Men*, released in 1939. Even with her success, they didn't renew Anna May's contract.

Tragedy struck the Wong family again in the summer of 1940. Anna May's sister Mary committed suicide. After mourning her sister's death, Anna May returned to work. She was cast in such films as *Bombs over Burma*, released in May 1942.

This is a film poster for *Island of Lost Men*.

Anna May didn't make any Hollywood movies for several years. Instead, she traveled. She embarked on a tour where she lectured on Chinese health and beauty. In 1949 Anna May returned to Hollywood, filming the movie, *Impact*. That year in October, her 89-year-old father died. Her dad and most of her family had returned to California in 1938. When her father died, Anna May felt a deep sense of loss. Although he had initially not supported her career choice over the years, he became one of Anna May's biggest supporters.

Because of positive reviews from her latest movie, Anna May decided to transition from movies to television. She was successful, landing her own show called *The Gallery of Madam Liu Tsong*. The half-hour Chinese detective series ran from August 27, 1951 through November 21. There was a rumored second series, scheduled to run in the spring of 1952 but the show was canceled.

Death and Legacy

In December 1953, Anna May had a health scare: she experienced internal bleeding. The doctors diagnosed her with Laennec's cirrhosis, an irreversible liver disease, usually caused by chronic alcoholism. After a few months recuperating in Pasadena, California, she returned to her house in Santa Monica.

Anna May returned to London in September 1955. She planned to remain in England longer, with jaunts to Paris and Munich, but because of finances, she returned to California in October. She decided to sell her property upon her return, as the area was being snapped up my real estate investors and she had an attractive corner lot.

Her health was okay, so she continued to work. She landed more television roles in the next few years, including an NBC show called *The Letter* and CBS' *The Climax Series,* both in 1956. She appeared in *Deadly Tattoo* in 1958, *Adventures in Paradise* the following year, and the *Wyatt Earp Show* in 1960.

In 1960 Anna May returned to the big screen, landing a small role in *Portrait in Black*. She was scheduled to begin filming a leading role in *Flower Drum Song*. Filming was scheduled for February 1961. Around Christmas, Anna May became ill with a "bug". By the first of the year, she was feeling better, but her health was shaky because of her liver disease. The director recast her role in *Flower Drum Song*.

On February 3, 1961, Anna May unexpectedly suffered a fatal heart attack. She was only 56 years old. Her funeral was held on February 8. In her will, Anna May requested cremation and to have her ashes placed near her mother's grave. And that's where she rests, at Rosedale Cemetery in Los Angeles.

Anna May Wong was the first Chinese-American movie star. She dreamed of becoming a Hollywood leading lady. She had the talent but was relegated to lesser roles because of Hollywood's ban on inter-racial kissing.

She made her mark in other ways. She was a fashion icon. She was successful at a young age in the United States and abroad. Still, she simply could not wiggle free from Hollywood's stereotypical roles.

Although she has remained largely forgotten, Anna May has received some recognition, especially in the Asian community. The Anna May Wong Award for Excellence given by the Asian-American Artists Foundation was named in her honor, for example.

Anna May paved the way for a new generation of Asian actors. These artists boast Chinese, Korean, Thai, Japanese, and other ethnic heritages. Actors like *The Walking Dead*'s Steven Yeun, *13 Reasons Why*'s Keiko Agena, and *Game of Throne*'s Rila Fukushima are part of a long list of popular Asian actors. Even if they don't realize it, Anna May opened the door so they could walk through.

Chapter Eight

Hattie McDaniel

Comedian, Singer, Actress

Humble Beginnings

For many African-American women during the early 1900s, career options were limited to low-paying domestic work. Hattie McDaniel wanted more from life and thought a career in entertainment was a way out.

Hattie was born June 10, 1893, the youngest child of Henry and Susan McDaniel. She was born in Wichita, Kansas and moved to Denver, Colorado when was five years old. Henry was a former slave who fought in the Civil War. Although he was a disabled veteran, the government refused to give him a pension for almost 20 years. Although he had proof that his injuries were sustained in the war, the government wouldn't budge. Former slaves often received worse treatment than their white counterparts. Susan also had health issues. Because of these factors, the family lived in poverty.

It was the second marriage for both parents. Susan had three children with her first husband: George, Addie, and Orleana (Lena). Both parents lost their spouses to death. On February 9, 1878, Hattie's parents married, and Henry embraced Susan's children as his own. The following year, the couple welcomed son, Hosea. Unfortunately, he died in infancy. Sons Ernest (1880; died in 1893), Otis (1882), and Samuel (1886) joined the family. Johnny was born in 1885 but died a few months later. Aidia (1886) died when she three. Mary, born in 1890, died within the week. Etta was born in 1891.

In Denver, Susan found domestic work with white families. She worked as a cook, nanny, and maid. Young Hattie sometimes accompanied her mother, where she learned how to cook, wash clothes, take care of kids, and serve meals.

Henry took odd jobs to feed his family, despite being in excruciating pain. In 1902, the government finally approved Henry's pension. It wasn't much — $6.00 a month (about $168.00 in 2018) but it helped the poverty-stricken family.

Even with his new pension, poverty followed the family like a menacing shadow. Author Jill Watts wrote in her book, *Hattie McDaniel: Black Ambition, White Hollywood* (2016), "The McDaniels could never quite beat poverty; they moved often and from one rental to another, mostly in and around Denver's segregated Five Points district."[127]

Hattie's parents' health continued to decline. Eventually Henry's eyesight was so poor, he was almost blind, and Susan's health made it impossible for her to work. In 1908, Henry, now 70 years old, requested a pension increase.

The government rejected his application because he couldn't prove his age, which was typical for former slaves without official birth records. Six years

---

127. Watts, 2016.

and a string of appeals later, Henry received an increase to $17.00 a month (about $419.00 in 2018).

First Taste of Fame

Otis was the first sibling to realize the potential for making money in the entertainment industry. In the early 1900s, he began performing and encouraged his younger siblings to join him. Otis, Etta, and Sam performed on Denver street corners. They sang and danced for tips. Later, Sam and four friends formed a group, called the "The Cakewalk Kids," and performed around town.

Otis wanted to do more than sing and dance: he wanted to produce original shows. In 1908, he wrote and produced a comedic play called *The Isles of Pingapoo or the Alabama Missionary.* The crowd loved the performance. Otis started performing in local theater productions and was high demand.

Hattie watched her older siblings from the sidelines and decided she wanted to perform. She was a good singer and dancer. When Hattie was eight years old, she performed for the first time at a carnival. She earned $5.00 (about $140.00 in 2018) in tips. Hattie started performing with her siblings after school and during the summer.

Growing up, Hattie's parents wanted their kids to get a decent education. Henry had basic reading and writing skills, while his wife was illiterate. Although the Denver school system was integrated, Hattie was one of two African-American students in her class at the 24th Street Elementary School.

Hattie enrolled in the East River High School in 1908. That year, Hattie had her first major performance. Along with siblings Otis and Etta, she appeared in a local variety show. Another family and a comedian also performed.

They show was a success. Local groups hired them for special events. Hattie also started performing solo. In 1909, she performed with a New York-based group, the Red Devils, during their stop in Denver. She also starred in Otis' musical comedy-drama, *J. William Johnson or Champion of Freedom.*

Hattie quit high school around this time to spend more time performing. In 1910, Otis formed a theatrical troupe. The company included Hattie. In April, they began touring across small-town-America. Sam formed a band and hit the road. The brothers soon decided to work together. They disbanded their separate groups, joined forces, and headed to Kansas City, Missouri.

Back at home, Hattie booked solo performances. But these were segregated times, so opportunities weren't knocking on her door. "Show business in general remained both dominated by men and extremely segregated," wrote Watts.[128]

When Hattie was 17 years old, she fell in love with a young man named Howard Hickman. Denver had a large poor African-American community, which Hattie was all too familiar with. It also had a black middle class. Howard's parents had decent jobs: his father was a railroad laborer and his mother had a federal job with the cleaning crew at the U.S. Post Office. Hattie married 21-year-old Howard on January 19, 1911. Her new husband was a skilled pianist who worked as a laborer during the day.

In May 1914, Hattie and Etta decided to start a production company. They created an all-female variety show to benefit a local women's organization, and it was a rousing success. The Denver community craved more from the McDaniels sisters. Soon the company was performing regularly, and Hattie became increasingly popular. In 1915, she began planning a

---

128. Watts, 2016.

solo performance. She set a date: March 4. But the show never happened. Howard became ill on February 22 and died from pneumonia on March 7. He was 26 years old, leaving Hattie a 21-year-old widow.

Hattie moved in with her parents. She withdrew from the entertainment business and temporarily resumed domestic work. After a year of mourning, Hattie returned to the stage in a play she wrote entitled, *Spirella Johnson from Memphis, Tennessee.*

The show was a sensation. It seemed life was looking rosier for the young widow, but it took a sharp turn downhill when her brother Otis died in November 1916. The siblings tried to move forward; Hattie and Etta began performing their variety show again. Hattie was a comedian, but she wanted more dramatic roles. Unfortunately, opportunities for African-American actresses were limited.

The McDaniel family soon experienced more grief: 70-year-old Susan McDaniel died in June 1920, followed by her husband in November 1922. Based on his acknowledged year of birth, he was 84 years old.

After their father's death, Etta decided to leave Denver for California. Life in Denver was becoming harder for African-Americans. "By 1923, the Ku Klux Klan was firmly ensconced in the city's power structure, dominating the police department and mayor's office and terrorizing the African-American population with bombings, cross burnings, and death threat," wrote Watts.[129]

Sam had settled in San Diego, where he had a popular jazz band. Etta stopped in San Diego but didn't stay long. She settled in Los Angeles. She

---

129. Watts, 2016.

found a steady job as a maid. She tried to make money performing but it was never enough.

Hattie remained in Denver. Her career wasn't going as planned, but she found love again. She remarried around 1922, although records are unclear of the exact date. Her marriage with Nym Lankfard was rocky from the start. Although accounts of what happened with the marriage vary, it's clear that Hattie eventually moved from her marital home into her family's house and kept her maiden name. It appears Lankfard left Denver shortly after the marriage, and the couple didn't live together again. The year they divorced is also unclear (either 1928 or 1938).

Hattie was still popular in the Denver African-American community, but she couldn't make a full-time salary performing. She got a break in 1924 when she was hired to work with a white-owned vaudeville company. Vaudeville troupes were traveling variety shows featuring a mix of comedy, singing, and dancing. She toured for five months. This was her first venture into white entertainment. The hours were long. Segregation was in full swing. Hotels refused to rent rooms to African-Americans. The company traveled by segregated trains.

Hattie's performance was usually well received. Her routine was a blend of comedy, blues singing, and dancing. After the success of the tour, Hattie was ready to finally leave Denver. Sam had joined Etta in Los Angeles. He was doing well in his career. His band still performed, and he had a radio gig on a weekly variety show called *Optimistic Do-Nuts,* playing a character he created named "Deacon McDaniel."

Chicago

Hattie didn't immediately join her siblings in California. She settled in Chicago and created a solo act. She accepted any offer that trickled her way for several years as she traveled the vaudeville circuit.

 Sometimes when Hattie accepted gigs, the organizers would flee without paying her. She ended up stranded and broke. Hattie would find domestic work until she earned enough money to get home.

During the summer of 1926, while performing her solo act in Kansas City, Missouri, Hattie teamed up with a talented pianist. Along with Hartzell "Tiny" Parham, Hattie wrote and recorded two songs for a local record label. Later that year, she made a recording with Lovie Austin's Blues Serenaders.

Hattie continued to perform domestic work to supplement her income. Then in 1927, she landed a job as a singer with Richard M. Jones and his Knights of Syncopation and went on tour with the band. Later, they recorded four of her songs for OKeh records. The company rejected one of the songs and never released the other three. In December, Hattie recorded with Tiny again. This time the record label approved two of her songs.

In April 1928, the family lost another member. Sister Addie died while Hattie was on the road. Not only was Hattie upset about the loss of her sister, but also was upset she couldn't attend the funeral.

Hattie continued to perform but struggled to make it big. She was offered a recording deal with Paramount Records in 1929, a significant step in her career. She recorded two songs with clarinetist Vance Dixon. She followed with two more recordings, this time with singer Papa Charlie Jackson.

That year, she got a small part in *Show Boat*, a musical by famed Broadway producer, Florence Ziegfeld. The show had a successful 15-week run in Chicago before hitting the road. Because of declining ticket sales and the cost of the elaborate show, Ziegfeld laid off some cast members, including Hattie.

She was stranded in Milwaukee, Wisconsin. Hattie found a job as a restroom attendant in a white nightclub. The pay was $7.00 a week (about $100.00 in 2018). One night the house band was desperate for a singer, so Hattie stepped in and saved the day with her soulful blues singing. She made $90.00 in tips (about $1,300.00 in 2018).

The owner hired Hattie as a regular singer. She headlined in the club for the next few years. In 1931, because of the failing economy, the club closed. Hattie was broke, and ready to leave Chicago for Hollywood.

 During the Great Depression of the 1930, African-Americans suffered more than white Americans. They were usually the first to lose their jobs. The rate of unemployment was two to three times higher in the black community.[130] The often received less aid than whites and were turned away from soup kitchens.

Hollywood

Sam introduced his sister to a friend, Harry, who managed vaudeville shows at a local theater. Harry Levette gave Hattie a shot, and the audience loved her solo performance.

Hattie next career move was the film industry. She met with casting agent Henry Butler. Butler's company, Cinema Exchanged, placed African-

---

130. Lynch, 2018.

American actors as extras and in small movie roles. In May 1931, Hattie landed her first gig, making $7.50 a day (about $122.00 in 2018) as an extra. During her first three years as an extra, she worked in over 100 movies.

Most of the roles weren't ideal. Jill Watts wrote that Hattie ". . . agreed to play stereotypes she had earlier lampooned, and ultimately participated in reinforcing American racist ideology on the silver screen."[131]

During Hattie's career, black actors were relegated to playing stereotypical roles like servants or criminals. Today, many African-American actors still struggle to land decent roles. Many are still cast in less desirable roles like criminals or secondary roles where their main purpose is emotional support for the white leading character.

Hattie continued performing in theater and landed singing gigs. In June 1931, she joined the Old Time Southern Singers, a group that performed African-American spirituals.

Sam talked to his boss at KNX radio. They agreed to give Hattie a spot on *Optimistic Do-Nuts*. She played three different characters. Hattie did so well, she was offered her own show. It was called *Hi Hat Hattie and Her Boys*.

She still had hopes of obtaining speaking movie roles. The wait was finally over when she was cast in *The Impatient Maiden* (1932). Her character was a woman hospitalized after a fight with her husband. Although the role wasn't stereotypical (a maid), Watts said it still ". . . was intended to play on white audiences' racist assumptions."[132]

---

131. Watts, 2016.
132. Watts, 2016.

Hattie continued to get small parts and some speaking roles. In *The Crooner* (1932), she played a singer. In *Washington Masquerade* (1932), she played a servant. She and Sam appeared in *The Golden West* (1932).

In the fall of 1933, she won the role of Queenie in a theatrical revival of *Show Boat*. This was Hattie's first major stage role. The show was a hit but plagued with problems: the company's treasurer was murdered during a robbery, and the original producer and theater owner owed back taxes. They sold their interest in the show and crept away with federal agents hot on their heels.

In January 1934, Hattie stepped away from her role. She was tired of the long hours and the financial problems hovering over the musical.

In May 1934, she received a one-picture contract. The movie was *Judge Priest* and Hattie's role was Aunt Dilcy, a housekeeper. It was significant because:

1. **The pay:** she earned $300.00 (about $5,500.00 in 2018);

2. **The role:** it was a speaking role *and* the character was in several scenes;

3. She received **onscreen credit**, although an 's' was added to her last name (a common error).

The role was formulaic: the character is subservient to her white employer, and she appears delighted in her position, literally singing and dancing while she works. After the movie was released, Hattie received good reviews. Other studios noticed her, and by the end of the year she had roles in eight more movies.

Hattie's biggest role to date came in late 1934, when she played the part of Mom Beck in *The Little Colonel*. The movie featured two popular stars: adorable kid actress Shirley Temple and talented black tap dancer, Bill "Bojangles" Robinson. Hattie played a servant; once again, the character was stereotypical.

Over the next few years, she landed more speaking roles. Reviews of her performance were favorable. In 1935, she was averaging about $250.00 a week (approximately $4,500.00 in 2018).

Her next big role was revising Queenie in the movie adaptation of *Show Boat,* which premiered in May 1936.

Hattie continued to work steadily. She purchased her first home. She was charitable to family friends, and strangers in need.

In 1937, Hattie found an agent. William Meiklejohn. He was one of the first white agents to represent black actors. Some of his clients became very successful, including Judy Garland and Lucille Ball. He also represented the future 40th U.S. President — Ronald Reagan.

Although Hattie continued to get roles mainly as servants, she played them as ". . . confident, assertive, and sassy," wrote Watts.[133]

Some in the African-American community criticized both Hollywood (for creating the characters) and Hattie (for accepting the roles). These characters perpetuated the myth of the obedient, happy-go-lucky servant, they argued.

---

133. Watts, 2016.

Gone With The Wind

Hattie is best known for playing the role of Mammy, in *Gone with the Wind*. The movie was based on the Pulitzer Prize-winning book of the same name. Written by Margaret Mitchell and published in 1936, the novel chronicles the demise of a white Southern family during and after the Civil War.

The central character is Scarlett O'Hara, a charming Southern belle. Scarlett only has eyes for Ashley Wilkes. You know the story: girl meets boy, war breaks out, girl marries some other dude.

The third central character is the charming but wicked Rhett Butler. Poor Scarlett (*literally*, her family becomes destitute after the war breaks out) eventually marries Rhett. No spoilers but let's just say the book doesn't exactly have a happy ending.

When it was announced producer David O. Selznick was making the book into a movie, African-American critics gave Selznick the stink eye. The book portrayed stereotypical black slaves, forever loyal to their masters. Even the name of the character "Mammy" was derogatory.

But Hattie was intrigued. She bought the book and devoured every page. After reading the book, she was sure she could bring a unique spin to the character. This would be her first major dramatic role.

It took Selznick two years to cast the lead characters. Hattie thought she was a long shot because of her previous comedic roles, but in January 1939, she signed her biggest contract to date — $450.00 a week (almost $8,000.00 in 2018). Clark Gable starred as Rhett, Vivien Leigh was Scarlett, and Leslie Howard played Ashley.

This is a screen grab of Hattie McDaniel and Vivien Leigh in *Gone with the Wind.*

Even before the film was released, opponents hounded Selznick. Letters poured into his office pleading with him to put the kibosh on the movie. Hattie received criticism for accepting the role.

The film premiered December 15, 1939. Selznick chose Atlanta for the premiere for two reasons: Mitchell was born in Atlanta and in homage to the book and movie's setting. Unfortunately, because of segregationist rules, Hattie and other black cast members were excluded from the Atlanta festivities. They attended a separate Hollywood premiere.

Hattie's portrayal of Mammy was not the same character in Mitchell's book. "She played the role with an astute quickness and vigor absent in Mitchell's pages," wrote Watts.[134]

---

134. Watts, 2016.

The movie and Hattie's performance received positive reviews. Some critics felt Hattie's character demeaned African-Americans, while others praised her performance. Supporters said she deserved an Academy Award. Selznick agreed. Hattie McDaniel became the first African-American actress nominated for the coveted award.

She was nominated in the "Best Supporting Actress" category. On February 29, 1940, Hattie became the first African-American actress to win an Oscar. You can find Hattie's Oscar emotional acceptance speech online here: **http://bit.ly/2C5GXeT.**

 You often see Academy Award and Oscar used interchangeably. Oscar is the nickname for the award. "Oscar" is the statuette the winner receives.

The next morning, Hattie was flooded with well wishes. The press praised her accomplishment — including many of her former critics. After her win, Hattie was certain Hollywood would bang on her door offering improved roles. But her contract with Selznick meant he controlled her career. He seemed content keeping her in the "Mammy" role.

Hattie's first movie after her win, *Maryland* (1940) was a step back, she said. She played a maid offering little more than comic relief. Hattie realized this was probably her fate.

In October 1940, Warner Brothers bought Hattie's contract from Selznick for $9,640.00 (about $180,000.00 in 2018). Selznick retained the option of using Hattie for one additional film each year.

Her first film with Warner was *The Great Lie*, starring Bette Davis. What was Hattie's role? You guessed it: she was a servant. In April 1941, the movie was released and received good reviews, but Hattie was growing weary of the same parts.

There was one bright spot in Hattie's life. She fell in love again. On March 21, 1941, she married an old friend from Chicago, James Crawford.

Finally, Hattie was cast in a better role. She played Minerva Clay in *In This Our Life,* once again alongside Bette Davis. Although Minerva is a maid, Hattie's scenes were more dramatic. Reviews were favorable, and specific mention was given of Hattie's performance.

The movie had racial undertones. In the film, Minerva's son is arrested and imprisoned for a crime he didn't commit. The crime was committed by one of the white characters. The son is arrested and jailed without any proof he committed the crime. In the end, the son is vindicated.

Hattie McDaniel, Chariman of the Negro Divison of the Hollywood Victory Committee, is seen here with fellow artists taking a break to perform at Minter Field circa 1941.

Hattie wasn't idle during World War II. She performed at United Service Organization (USO) shows, for example. The USO provides entertainment to U.S. military service members. Her movie career was stagnant. In 1942, she made two movies; both characters were stereotypical comic relief. In the summer of 1942, Warner and Hattie reached an agreement. They released her from her contract with an obligation to do three more films. After her release, Hattie struggled to find decent roles.

In May 1944, Hattie had a big announcement: she was pregnant with her first child at 51 years old. Unfortunately, it was a false pregnancy. This occurs when a woman believes she's expecting because she has pregnancy symptoms.

Her sorrows continued. In April 1945, James Crawford left her, and Hattie filed for divorce in August. But wait, there's more. Hattie had purchased her home in a neighborhood that normally restricted African-Americans from buying property. Unless white homeowners protested, these sales weren't problematic. In the summer of 1945, eight of Hattie's white neighbors decided to file a lawsuit to have her evicted.

 The process of not allowing African-Americans to purchase property in white neighborhoods was called a "restrictive covenant."

Although she played docile servants in film, Hattie was the opposite in real life. She refused to give up her home without a fight. She gathered black neighbors facing the same legal problem. Superior Court Judge Thurmond Clarke heard the case in December 1945. In a surprise decision, Judge Clarke ruled restrictive covenants were unconstitutional. Hattie could keep her home.

Good news was followed by bad. In January 1946, Hattie's beloved sister Etta died. Hattie was understandably shaken. The sisters had been extremely close. That same year Hattie appeared in only four films, most notably Disney's *Song of the South*, an innovative movie featuring animation and live action. Hattie was Aunt, just another happy, wisecracking servant.

Beulah

Hattie found success in radio, though. CBS radio had a weekly program called *Beulah*. The title character was a black female maid but was voiced by white male actor, Marlin Hurt. This was a common practice in radio during that time. In 1946, Hurt died. Another white male, Bob Corley replaced him, but the producers weren't happy with his performance.

Because the show had been successful years, CBS didn't want to end it. They decided to audition African-American females to take over the role. Hattie landed the role. Her first episode aired in November 1947.

This is a photo of Hattie McDaniel playing Beulah for CBS.

Hattie's presence revived the sinking ship. Proctor & Gamble, the show's sponsor, saw a way to make more money. Hattie would be the voice *and* face of *Beulah*. Hattie (as Beulah) appeared in TV commercials and print ads. The show was so popular it went from weekly to five days a week. Hattie received $1,500.00 a week (about $17,000.00 in 2018).

Hattie also found love again with Larry Williams, a popular interior decorator. Hattie was 53 years old; Larry was 40 years old. They hit it off and Hattie walked down the aisle again on June 11, 1949. Ah, but there was no wedded bliss.

You've probably heard of a pre-nuptial agreement (pre-nup). Well, after the wedding, Hattie asked her husband to sign a post-nup, relinquishing any claims to her assets. From there, the couple argued about everything. They even bickered in public. Four months after the couple said, "I do," Williams said, "I'm out!"

Hattie filed for divorce in December 1950. During this time, she started feeling unhealthy. She thought maybe she was working too hard on *Beulah*. She decided to slow down. She took Sundays off to chill and decided to eat healthier. But these efforts didn't energize Hattie.

After fighting to keep her home, Hattie sold it. She bought a smaller one with rooms all on the same floor (she had trouble climbing stairs). She was able to continue working though.

She got a *big* break February 1951. The previous year, ABC decided to bring *Beulah* to television. This was a *big* deal; no black actress had starred in her own television series. However, they didn't cast Hattie in the staring role. Instead, the role went to Ethel Waters, whose portrayal was a flop. In February 1951, ABC remedied their first mistake and offered the role to

Hattie. She would now do double duty as Beulah. She filmed six episodes while the radio version was on summer break.

This is a photo of Hattie McDaniel playing both the voice and face of Beulah for ABC.

Death and Legacy

In August, Hattie's brother found her on the floor of her house. She couldn't speak or move. The diagnosis was tragic and the outlook grim: a stroke, advanced heart disease, and diabetes.

ABC re-cast Hattie's role in *Beulah*. CBS ran reruns of the radio broadcast. She remained in the hospital for two months before being well enough to return home. She assured the press she would recover. In December, she made out her will, just in case. Sam would receive most of her estate. She willed her Oscar to Howard University. She left Larry Williams $1.

What Happened to Hattie McDaniel's Oscar?

No one knows for sure what happened to Hattie's coveted award. After her death, it was displayed at Howard's fine arts complex. It's believed the Oscar disappeared in the late 1960s or early 1970s. This was during a time of student protests on the campus.

Some theorize it was purposefully thrown away. The Black Power movement was at its height. Some suggest because of the roles Hattie accepted, a student(s) was upset and chucked the Oscar. Others suggest it may simply have been thrown away by mistake or misplaced.

Hattie was able to get out of bed in April 1952 but relapsed quickly. The doctors added another diagnosis: advanced breast cancer. Because of the disease's progression, treatment wasn't an option.

With mounting medical bills and unable to work, Hattie sold her house. She moved into the Motion Picture Country Home. She hoped for a miracle, but her body couldn't fight the many ailments invading it. Hattie

McDaniel died October 26, 1952, two days after slipping into a coma. She was 57 years old.

Hattie had requested a modest funeral. Sam planned to honor her wishes but many people wanted to pay their respects, so he decided to have a larger public service. The funeral was held Nov. 1 and an estimated 5,000 people attended the service.

Hattie McDaniel was buried in the Rosedale Cemetery in Los Angeles with a simple headstone: **Hattie McDaniel, 1895-1952**.

 Hattie's estate was estimated at only about $10,000 (about $93,000 in 2018) when she died. Creditors and the Internal Revenue Service gobbled up most of what was left.

Most of Hattie's awards came after her death. She has two stars on the Hollywood Walk of Fame. In 1975, she was inducted into the Black Film-makers Hall of Fame. In 2006, the U.S. Postal Service issued a stamp in her likeness as part of the *Black Heritage Series*.

Although she never received the dramatic roles she felt she deserved, Hattie McDaniel left a legacy of inspiration. Ridiculed by some and dismissed by others because of the types of roles she was willing to take, she was an inspiration to countless African-American aspiring actors.

Although the Academy has been stingy in awarding black performers, a few have received the coveted Oscar. *This* is Hattie's legacy:

- **2017: Viola Davis** — Best Supporting Actress, *Fences*

- **2017: Mahershala Ali** — Best Supporting Actor, *Moonlight*

- **2013: Lupita Nyong'o** — Best Supporting Actress, *12 Years a Slave*

- **2012: Octavia Spencer** — Best Supporting Actress, *The Help*

- **2009: Mo'Nique** — Best Supporting Actress, *Precious*

- **2006: Forrest Whitaker** — Best Actor, *The Last King of Scotland*

- **2006: Jennifer Hudson** — Best Supporting Actress, *Dreamgirls*

- **2004: Morgan Freeman** — Best Supporting, Actor *Million Dollar Baby*

  2004: Jamie Foxx — Best Actor, *Ray*

- **2002 and 1989: Denzel Washington** — Best Actor, *Training Day* and Best Supporting Actor, *Glory*

- **2001: Halle Berry Best** — Actress, *Monster's Ball*

- **1996: Cuba Gooding, Jr.** — Best Supporting Actor, *Jerry McGuire*

- **1991: Whoopi Goldberg** — Best Supporting Actress, *Ghost*

- **1982: Louis Gossett, Jr.** — Best Supporting Actor *An Officer and a Gentleman*

- **1963: Sidney Poitier** — Best Actor, *Lilies of the Field*

Chapter Nine

International Sweethearts of Rhythm

Swing Sisters

Swing Sisters

Each of the previous chapters focused on one extraordinary female artist. Chapter 9 highlights a talented group of female musicians: The International Sweethearts of Rhythm, who broke gender and racial barriers in the music world during the 1940s. They were the first all-female, integrated girl band. Despite their popularity and talent, their story has received sparse attention.

Let's start where all good stories start — at the beginning.

Piney Woods

The story of the Sweethearts begins in rural Mississippi at the Piney Woods Country Life School. The small town of Piney Woods is about 21 miles south of Jackson, Mississippi. Dr. Laurence C. Jones established the school in 1909. He founded the Christian boarding school to provide a decent education to poor and orphaned — mostly African-American — children.

The inaugural class had three students. At the beginning of the second year, there were 100.

 Based on self-reported data, the rate of illiteracy in 1900 was about 30.5 percent (blacks) and 6.2 percent (whites).[135] The rate in 2017 was approximately 9 percent for whites and 24 percent for African-Americans[136].

Dr. Jones started the school with $2 on land donated by a former slave. He met opposition from whites in the community, including Mississippi governor, James Vardaman, a known white supremacist. However, some white businesses offered support. For example, the owner of a sawmill donated lumber for building renovations.

Many of the teachers Dr. Jones hired were retired white teachers from the North. They weren't paid; instead, they received room and board.

 Dr. Jones, a University of Iowa graduate, was only 26 years old when he founded Piney Woods.

In addition to academics, the students learned vocational or trade skills, like sewing, shorthand, typing, or carpentry. There was also lots of music. The school was known for its two male jazz bands. Another all-girl female band was the impetus for the formation of the Sweethearts.

"My father heard the band over the radio one time and said, 'I've got a lot of girls here. Maybe I could start myself an all-girl band,' " recalled Dr. Jones' daughter, Helen.[137]

135. Snyder, 1993.
136. Statistics Brain Research Institute, 2017.
137. McDonough, 2011.

Like the other bands, the new group would perform to raise money for the school. Some of the parents didn't like the idea of the girls playing jazz or swing because of the religious nature of the school, but Dr. Jones was able to get enough girls from the existing marching band and other interested students to create his ensemble.

Piney Woods Country Life School Today

They may have dropped the "Country Life" from the name of the school, but Piney Woods continues to operate as a boarding school with a focus on academic excellence. The co-educational school's student body comes from over 20 different states. They also have many international students. The student population is diverse, and tuition assistance is available. The current (as of February 2018) president, Will Crossley is the fifth president and first alumni to lead the 107-year-old institution.

The school offers a robust curriculum, an athletic department, clubs and organizations, college prep programs, and a summer youth leadership institute. Each student participates in an on-campus work-study program and religious activities. The school had 118 students in grades 9-12 during the 2015-2016 school year.

The Sweethearts was organized in 1937. One of the original members was Dr. Jones' daughter, Helen.

The band had three sections:

Brass — *trumpets and trombones*

Woodwind — *clarinets and saxophones*

Rhythm — *drums, piano, bass, guitars*

Consuella Carter was the girls' music teacher. Most of the Sweethearts didn't have any or much musical background. But with hours of practice, they learned to play as if they'd been born with the instrument in their hands.

When the Sweethearts traveled, Miss Crawford, their tutor made sure the girls didn't fall behind in their academics. At one point, they had two buses. One was for traveling and sleeping; the other was their "school bus." The girls ranged in age from 13 to 16 years old.

 Swing was called "Big Band Music" because of the large number of musicians in the band.

The band eventually grew to 18 members. The original members of the band were:

Evelyn McGhee - *vocalist*

Pauline Braddy - *drums*

Willie Mae Wong - *saxophone*

Alma Cortez - *saxophone and clarinet*

Helen Jones - *trombone*

Johnnie Mae Rice - *piano*

Irene Grisham - *saxophone*

Ilone Grisham - *saxophone*

Judy Bayron - *trombone*

The young ladies quickly became popular. They played at church, school, and other community events. In a short time, the band was raising about $3,000 a month for the school (about $50,000.00 in 2018).

Popular male musicians like Cab Calloway, Duke Ellington, and Dizzy Gillespie praised the Sweethearts skills. The women participated in "Battle of the Bands" and usually did well, sometimes better than the male bands.

Spotlight on: Helen Jones Woods *(b. 1923)*
Trombone

Helen was born in Meridian, Mississippi in 1923. Her exact date of birth is unknown because she was an orphan. Dr. Jones and his wife Grace adopted Helen. She was initially placed in a white orphanage because of her fair skin. When they realized she was black, she was removed. When Helen was four years old, Grace unexpectedly died.

Helen was originally part of another school band, the Cotton Blossom Singers. When the Sweethearts disbanded, Helen moved to Omaha and married William Woods. He became the first African-American student to earn an accounting degree from Creighton University. The couple had four children. Helen was a licensed practical nurse (LPN) for 23 years before retiring in 1970. In 2007, she was inducted into the Omaha Black Music Hall of Fame.

International Sweethearts

As their popularity soared, so did tensions between the Sweethearts and Piney Woods. It was rumored that money was the source of the friction. Members earned $8.00 a week (about $135.00 in 2018); the remainder went to the school. Some of the young ladies severed ties with Piney Woods in 1941. They moved to Arlington, Virginia and began their professional career. They found a new musical director/arranger, Eddie Durham, who had worked with the great Count Basie.

The got a new lead singer and bandleader, Anna Mae Winburn. When asked to join the group, she recalled thinking: "What a bunch of cute little girls but I don't know whether I can get along with that many women or not."[138] Thankfully, she did and went on to lead this talented group of musicians.

---

138. Schiller, 1986.

 Eventually the girls received a salary increase to about $15.00 a week (around $200.00 in 2018)

The "International" tag reflected the racial makeup of the young ladies. Members included African-American, Asian, Mexican, Native American, and white musicians. The sweethearts traveled with a manager, Rae Lee Jones, their former Piney Woods chaperone. The band often performed "one-nighters". They would play in a city one night, then hop on the tour bus and travel hundreds of miles for a gig in another city the following night.

This is a lobby card for a the American musical film *That Man of Mine* (1946).

Spotlight on: Anna Mae Winburn
(August 13, 1913- September 30, 1999)
Vocals/ Bandleader

Anna Mae was born in Port Royal, Tennessee but moved to Kokomo, Indiana when she was young. She began singing with the band for WOWO radio in Fort Wayne, Indiana. From there, she performed in clubs in Indiana and Indianapolis.

After moving to North Omaha, Nebraska, she continued singing and playing guitar with local bands. Before joining the Sweethearts, Anna Mae was the vocalist for several male bands including Lloyd Hunters Serenaders and the Cotton Club Boys of Omaha.

She joined the band in 1942 and remained with the Sweethearts until the end. After the Sweethearts disbanded, Anna Mae sang with different bands for several years, none of which were as successful as the Sweethearts. Winburn married Eustace Pilgrim in 1948, and they had four children. She lived in Elmhurst, New York until she died when she was 86 years old.

Musicians cycled in and out of the group. The first white musician, saxophonist Rosalind "Roz" Cron, joined the Sweethearts in 1943. Trumpeter Toby Butler joined that same year.

While black communities and Northern whites welcomed the group, playing in the segregated South was different. According to Cron, she didn't notice any difference when playing in cities like New York or Chicago. But in the Deep South, ". . . her presence was criminal."[139]

Cron and other white band members had to take measures to keep themselves and the other members safe. They wore dark makeup to appear black.

---

139. McDonough, 2011.

They were instructed to say they were bi-racial if questioned by police. It might seem silly today, but during the Jim Crow era, blacks and whites hanging out together was frowned upon, and in some cases illegal. The possibility of physical violence was real. To avoid problems in the South, they slept on the bus. They couldn't rent hotel rooms together anyway. They also ate on the bus, as most restaurants wouldn't serve them.

 The Sweethearts tour bus was nicknamed "Big Bertha."

One time while performing in the South, three white members had to slip out the back of the bus because someone reported them to the police. By the time the police arrived, the three young ladies had gotten into a cab and sped away to the train station.

Roz related another scary Deep South incident. One night following a show in El Paso, Texas, the Sweethearts were headed to the local café. Roz was delayed by a group of kids curious about the reeds she used when playing the saxophone. She took time to answer their questions and when she was finished, a black solider offered to walk with her to the café.

A sheriff's car began circling Roz and the soldier. "One got out and he's got the usual ten

gallon hat which made him a foot taller and the boots with the heels and he was just overwhelming and he wanted to know where we were going and what we were doing," Roz recalled.[140]

---

140. Smithsonian, 2011.

The sheriffs took Roz and soldier to jail. They yelled at the soldier for a while before telling him to leave town and never return. They threw Roz in a cell for half the night until her "cousin" Helen Jones sprang her out.

The Sweethearts became such a sensation that people waited in long lines to see them perform. During a one-week engagement at the Howard Theater in Washington, D.C, a record-setting 35,000 people saw the band perform.

Some of the places they performed include:

- **The Apollo Theater, Regal Theater**, and **Savoy Ballroom** (New York)

- **The Cotton Club** (Cincinnati, Ohio)

- **The Riviera** (St. Louis, Missouri)

- **The Dreamland** (Omaha, Nebraska)

- **The Million Dollar** (Los Angeles, California)

Sometimes the Sweethearts were the featured house band. They backed up great performers like Ella Fitzgerald and Billie Holliday. If you want to hear the Sweethearts, there are several clips online. Here's a good one to check out: **https://youtu.be/WczP3PyHt20.**

Spotlight on: Pauline Braddy Williams
(February 14, 1922 - January 28, 1996)
Drummer

Pauline was born in Mendenhall, Mississippi. At Piney Woods, she started playing the clarinet. She wanted to play the saxophone but ended up becoming the drummer when the original musician dropped out. She was a talented and powerful drummer. She was called "Queen of the Drums." Some say her drum skills helped make the Sweethearts the successful band they were.

When the Sweethearts disbanded, Pauline moved to New York, where she continued to work as a drummer, working with the Vi Burnside All-Stars, the Edna Smith Trio, and Two Plus One. She moved to Washington to take care of her ailing mother in the 1960s. She settled into a career as a switchboard operator. She was twice married but both unions ended in divorce. After she retired in 1994, she moved to Braxton, Mississippi. Pauline died of flu complications. She was 73 years old.

As one of the few all-female bands at the time, some people didn't take them seriously. They were called a novelty act, which the ladies disliked. Their pay was below their male counterparts. They were just as good, sometimes better than male bands. Famous male bands at the time included Louis Armstrong and Count Basie.

It *was* unusual (if novelty is offensive) for women to play "Big Band" instruments. Women usually played the piano, strings, violin, and cello. Women *did not* play bass, saxophone, or trumpets! Those were male instruments.

The Sweethearts sometimes received backhand compliments like: "They play okay for a girl band." Some male musicians did compliment them (sort of) by saying they played like men. Some of the male bands ignored them.

During World War II, many male musicians went off to fight, which gave the group opportunities to play.

 In 1944 *DownBeat* magazine named the Sweethearts "America's #1 All-Girl Orchestra".

Probably their most exciting performance was a European tour during World War II. The African-American soldiers requested the band and they were happy to entertain the troops. In 1945, they embarked on six-month USO tour. They traveled to France, Belgium, and Germany. The Sweethearts reportedly had a great time traveling abroad. They were well received (and much appreciated) by the soldiers.

The End of an Era

After men returned from war, the Sweethearts began losing gigs. The women returned to or started new careers. Many of the male musicians returning from war, snatched up available gigs. The Big Band era was also ending.

The new sound was bebop jazz with smaller bands. Rhythm and Blues (R&B) was becoming more popular in the black community. In 1947 Rae Lee Jones died. This may have been the last nail in the Sweethearts' coffin. After a 10-year run, the International Sweethearts of Rhythm disbanded.

Spotlight on: Ernestine Carroll ("Tiny" Davis)
(August 5, 1909 - January 30, 1994)
Trumpet

Sometimes people earn their nicknames because of certain features, which are the opposite. Such was the case for full-figured "Tiny" Davis. She was born in Memphis, Tennessee on August 5, 1909. She began playing the trumpet because she saw boys in her high school playing the unknown instrument and she wanted one too. She asked her mother to buy her a trumpet and she obliged. She quickly became a sensational player. She could also sing.

Tiny later moved Kansas City with her husband. She began playing for a few dollars in the local clubs. This was around 1935. She played with the Harlem Playgirls before joining the Sweethearts in 1943. She was one of the bands favorite and most talented performers. "I brought in the crowds," she said. "I was wild, loud and fat . . ."[141]

She was so talented, Louis Armstrong tried to pry her away from the Sweethearts, but she refused. She was even called "The Female Louis Armstrong." Tiny eventually separated from her husband and moved to St. Louis, Missouri. While still in Kansas, she started a relationship with fellow musician Ruby Lucas. The couple remained together for over 40 years.

After the Sweethearts disbanded, Tiny started her own successful band, Tiny Davis and Her Hell Divers. The couple had a successful club, Tiny and Ruby's Gay Spot, in the 1950s. Tiny died in Chicago was 85 years old.

Legacy

It took two decades after the group disbanded before interest in the Sweethearts returned. This was during the Women's Liberation Movement in the 1960s and 1970s. This new interest may have paved the way for talented female jazz musicians to pursue their musical passions.

---

141. Schiller, 1996.

"Sadly, the Sweethearts' surviving footprint in jazz history remains as tiny as Snow White's slipper: only five commercial records, a few Soundie films and about a dozen broadcast performances (all gathered on a single CD, Hot Licks)," wrote John McDonough in a 2011 article for *DownBeat* magazine ("Honoring Jazz's Historic Sweethearts").[142]

McDonough admits the very magazine he works for wasn't much help in spreading the word about the Sweethearts and other female musicians in the 1930s and 40s. He pointed to a February 1938 article, "Why Women Musicians Are Inferior," as proof. Today, they probably would have gotten a lot more attention and recognition through social media.

One group that *has* gotten attention is the Diva Jazz Orchestra. This popular all-female jazz band has been performing since 1993. The 15-member ensemble recorded 12 albums and toured across the United States and internationally.

Cathy Hughes

Dr. Jones' granddaughter, Cathy Hughes, is the founder of Urban One (formally Radio One). The media empire is the largest African-American owned and operated broadcast company in the nation. In 1999, Hughes took her company public, selling more than seven million shares of common stock. This move made her the first African-American women to head a publicly held company. Hughes runs Urban One with her son and business partner Alfred Liggins, III.

The company has several subsidiaries, including TV One, which features the hit shows *R & B Divas* and *UnSung*. Reach Media is the home of popular radio programs the *Rickey Smiley Morning Show* and *Tom Joyner Morning Show*. The company also owns Interactive Once, home to websites including *The Daily Grind* and *Hello Beautiful* and a marketing firm (One Solution).

---

142. McDonough, 2011.

The Sweethearts faced racial and gender bias while simply trying to make a joyful noise. Despite these barriers, they survived for a decade as the hottest, most talented female jazz band of their generation. In 1980, some of the women came together for the first time since they disbanded. They were honored at Women's Jazz Festival. They were honored again in 2011, this time by the Smithsonian. Hopefully, a new generation will learn about the Sweethearts and realize that with hard work and determination, they too can achieve their musical dreams.

Chapter Ten

Lakshmi Shankar

Dance Was My First Love

Lakshmi Shankar's name is not as well known as her brother-in-law, Ravi Shankar. In many ways, she appears as merely a footnote on the pages of his life story as a Shankar family member.

But Lakshmi Shankar was talented singer in her own right who never received the widespread recognition she deserved outside her native country. By all accounts, Lakshmi was had one of the best classical Hindustani (North Indian) voices of all times.

She was born Lakshmi Sastri on June 16, 1926 in Jamshedpur, India. She began singing when she was three but received formal training in dance. When she was eight years old, she began training in *Bharatanatyam*, a classical Indian dance. "Dance was my first love . . ." she said in an interview published in 2001.[143]

---

143. Isal, 2001.

Her mother Visalakshi was a singer and short story writer. Her dad, Pudukkottai R. Viswanatha, edited the Indian activist Mahatma Gandhi's journal, *The Harijan*.

Her life with the Shankar family began in 1939. Nine years earlier, Uday Shankar founded a Paris-based dance company, *Compaigne de Danse et Musique Hindou* (Company of Hindu Music and Dance). Uday was the older brother of Rajendra Shankar, Lakshmi's future husband.

When the teenage Lakshmi met the troupe, she decided she wanted to join the group as a dancer. She applied and was accepted as a member of the Uday Shankar India Culture Center in Almora.

"The Almora Center was a most wonderful institution and I wish it had lasted longer," Lakshmi said in a 2010 interview.[144]

"The four years I spent there was the most fantastic time in my life, I had the best of everything and I am thankful to God for giving it to me. We not only learned music and dance but so many other things in life that have guided us through," she added.[145]

Lakshmi married Rajendra Shankar in 1941. She was 15 years old; he was decades older. After the center closed in 1944, the couple moved to Bombay (now Mumbai), where Rajendra worked as a scriptwriter.

Shattered Dreams and a New Love

In 1947, Lakshmi's hopes of being a great dancer ended when she developed pleurisy. This painfully debilitating disease is caused when the thin

---

144. Pai, 2010.
145. Pai, 2010.

layers (called pleura) that covers the wall of the lungs become inflamed. The inflammation can cause severe chest pain and difficulty breathing.

 Lakshmi is the Hindu goddess of wealth.

A painted depiction of the Hindu goddess, Lakshmi.

She had just finished her last performance playing the lead ballet role in *The Discovery of India*, choreographed and produced by the Shankar brothers. Her doctor told her she would never dance again. "My dreams were shattered," she said.[146]

---

146. Isal, 2001.

After Lakshmi recovered, she started helping her husband. She learned shorthand and typing. She did some singing and acting in local films. She was an early Bollywood actress. Bollywood is the Indian film industry. The name derives from a mash up of Bombay (now Mumbai) and Hollywood. Ravi said she had the voice for classical music and encouraged her to begin voice training.

The couple had two children. Their first child, Vijayashree (Viji), was born in 1952. She was a gifted singer and often performed with her mother. She was married to the classical violinist L. Subramaniam. Viji died of cancer in 1995.

Son Kumar said he and his sister grew up in a house filled with music. "She would practice for hours and hours each day . . . we were surrounded by music all the time," he said.[147]

Ravi Shankar

He was born Ravindra Shankar Chowdhury April 7, 1920 in Benares, India. He was known for playing the sitar, a stringed instrument popular in Hindustani music. He was also a composer, and founder of the National Orchestra of India, the Kinnara School of Music in Bombay and in Los Angeles.

He's probably best known for introducing Indian music to the Western world, thanks in part to his collaboration with the Beatles George Harrison. During his long career, he received numerous accolades, including four Grammy Awards (one given two months after his death). The Shankar family of talented musicians includes Shankar's daughter, Norah Jones. Jones is an award-winning singer whose work blends country with jazz and pop.

Ravi Shankar died December 11, 2011 in San Diego, California.

---

147. Tsering, 2014.

Ravi Shankar in Delhi, 2009.

Lakshmi first began singing Carnatic music, which is the traditional music of southern India. After she began her classical training, she became a master of the Hindustani khyals and thumris. A khyal is improvised and emotional. This form "... consists of around 4-8 lines of lyrics set to a tune. The singer then uses these few lines as the basis for improvisation," according to a description on the New World Encyclopedia's website.[148]

Thumris are considered semi-classical and use romantic lyrics. She was also a master of the bhajans, which use religious or spiritual lyrics. Lakshmi could sing in 14 different languages, including Tamil, Hindi, and Bengali.

---

148. New World Encyclopedia, 2017.

"When I sing I see the expression and the movement of the words and feel them as a dancer would," she once explained.[149]

She began training in 1954 with Ustad Abdul Rehman Khan, singing four hours a day for the next three years.

 Khan was Lakshmi's *guru* or teacher; she was his *shishya* or student.

Lakshmi's first public recital was in 1957 at a music conference in Calcutta. She received a medal for outstanding performance. She continued singing in India, and then she had an opportunity to travel abroad. She was the first Indian vocalist to perform outside India.

During 1962-1963, Lakshmi performed in the United States, Canada, and Europe with Uday Shankar. She returned to the United States again 1968 to tour with Ravi's "Festival from India" ensemble. In 1970, she performed solo in Florence, Venice, and Rome, Italy. Lakshmi also performed at the Shiraz Festival in Iran during this time. During the "Shankar Family & Friends" tours in the 1970s (which spawned an album of the same name), Viji, Lakshmi, and her sister, Kamala, were the only three females performers.

Working with her brother-in-law Ravi, Lakshmi gained popularity not only in her native India, but also in the United States. In 1974, Lakshmi toured with Ravi and ex-Beatles George Harrison as the lead singer for the "Music Festival from India." The group — which included many members of the Shankar family — toured in Europe and North America.

When Ravi suffered a heart attack in Chicago during the tour, Lakshmi conducted the orchestra for the next nine performances.

---

149. Tsering, 2014.

Lakshmi was also featured on the soundtrack of the 1982 movie *Gandhi*. Ravi composed all except two of songs on the movie's soundtrack.

Death and Legacy

Lakshmi moved to Los Angeles in 1983, after her husband died the previous year. She continued to make annual trips to India to visit Kamala until her sister moved away. Both of her kids had already moved to Los Angeles. "Within a few years, I became more recognized, my albums came out and I started performing full length concerts just like I had done in India," she said.[150]

She retired from performing in 2008, and began teaching full-time. She was a master teaching artist at the Alliance for California Traditional Arts apprentice program in 2010 and 2012, where she trained the next generation of Indian vocalists. She also taught briefly at the Ali Akbar Khan College of Music & Dance.

Lakshmi died December 30, 2013 in Simi Valley, California. She was 87 years old. In her lifetime, Lakshmi received a few honors including:

- A 2009 Grammy nomination for her album *Dancing in the Light*
- A Durfee Foundation Grant to teach Indian music to American students
- A "Woman of the Year" Kalpana Chawla Award
- A Bengali Association of New York Lifetime Achievement Award
- An Award from Sri Chinmoy for "Uplifting the World with Music"

---

150. Pai, 2010.

A statement from her family after her death stated:

"She had a heavenly voice which would melt any heart. She was a kind and beautiful soul. We will miss her."[151]

Some of her family members have remarked that Lakshmi never received the honors she deserved. Her granddaughter Gingger Shankar attributed this oversight to the ". . . male-oriented nature" of the family."[152] A talented musician herself, Gingger played the violin on Katy Perry's *Prism* album. She performed with the group The Smashing Pumpkins. She was featured on the soundtrack of *The Passion of the Christ* (2004).

The first biography of the talented singer is scheduled for release in April 2018. Davita Kas, who was friends with the singer, wrote *Poignant Song: The Life and Music of Lakshmi Shankar*, to finally tell Lakshmi's story.

"I'm excited about the opportunity to tell Lakshmi's story because I believe she provides a perspective on the journey of Indian music to the West that has rarely been heard from: a female Indian musician who was part of that movement," Kas wrote in 2013.[153]

Again, much of her legacy seems intertwined with that of the Shankar family, specifically the male members. Her participation in introducing the western world to Indian music cannot be understated. Although her gifted daughter died young, we hear her influence in her descendants including Gingger and the younger generation of Shankar offsprings.

---

151. Tsering, 2014.
152. Faizal, 2016.
153. Kas, 2013.

The women highlighted in this book achieved success in their respective artistic endeavors, but they never truly received the recognition they deserved. Perhaps they were victims of the times they lived in. Maybe they were hindered by racial or gender discrimination. We may never know. Hopefully, this book has achieved its goal of informing a new generation about these great women.

Many of these women have been written out of the history books or appear as a blurb, sometimes in relation to males. Lakshmi Shankar, for example, was often referred to as "the sister-in-law" of Ravi. Maria Tallchief's success was often attributed to George Balanchine's ability to mold and shape her career as a dancer. Winnie Davis' legacy is as the Daughter of the Confederacy. Her skills as a gifted writer have been dismissed.

However, it's important to learn about these trailblazing women. Despite the stumbling blocks placed in their path, they still achieved success in their respective fields. They pressed on and moved forward. They didn't regret their decision to pursue their passion.

Today, young girls are taught they can have a family *and* a successful career. This wasn't the case for the women we've discussed. Some were taught marriage and motherhood was the ultimate goal. A career, especially in the arts field, was secondary to home and family. Or, if they chose to pursue a professional path, they often had to forgo a happy domestic life.

Thanks to these trailblazing women and many others, young ladies know success is within reach. They simply have to work hard and follow their dreams.

This book presents a small glimpse into the lives of these amazing women. I hope you'll be motivated to learn more about them. Spend some time reading Winnie's books or gazing at Edmonia or Romaine's work online (or in person, if possible). You can find clips of prima ballerina Maria Tallchief and Queen of the Gypsies Carmen Amaya online. Why not grab some snacks and have a movie night featuring Hattie and Anna May?

The women highlighted in this book are a small sample of women hidden from history. There are countless phenomenal women waiting to be discovered. Hopefully this book has whet your appetite, and you'll spend some time discovering more of these buried gems.

When I began writing this book, I had no idea how much I would learn. Of all the artists featured, the only person I was familiar with was Hattie McDaniel, and that knowledge was limited.

I wanted to write this book because I was curious about the artistic women wiped from the pages of history. I didn't expect to get so wrapped up in their lives. As I conducted my research, I was drawn deeper into their sorrows and successes. I began to see similarities and connections between some of the women.

Hattie and Anna May, for example, are buried in the same Los Angeles cemetery. Both wanted to become big movie stars but Hollywood seemed content on casting them in stereotypical roles. Both women were rumored to have had bi-sexual relationships. Was this just juicy gossip or were the women in the closet? We don't know. We do know that Romaine and the Sweetheart's Tiny Davis were proud lesbians and lovingly embraced by the gay community.

We also have fashion icons/influencers Amelia, Anna May, and Romaine. A couple of our women married often. That would be Hattie and Maria, in case you forgot. Hattie and Anna May had their last roles recast due to health issues.

The women traveled often and some chose to become expatriates living abroad. I was intrigued by the mysteries I discovered. What happened to Edmonia Lewis when she dropped off the radar? What happened to Hattie's coveted Oscar?

Of course, the women had their differences. Some of these women were blessed to live long lives. Others had their lives cut short. Some of the women were born into poverty and others were born with silver spoons in their mouth.

They came from large and small families. Some became orphaned at a young age, while others lost their parents in adulthood. Most had the support of their loved ones, as they chased their dreams.

The one thing I learned from writing this book is how fierce and unafraid these women were. Their stories inspired me, and I hope they have inspired you.

Archivist *a person in charge of collecting, organizing, and maintaining records*

Pseudonym *a false name, sometimes used by writers*

Diphtheria *a bacterial infection that causes thick mucus to build in the throat or nose and makes it hard to breath or swallow*

Yellow fever *a disease caused by a virus, which is spread by mosquito bites*

Patriarch *the male head of a family*

Infidelity the act of being unfaithful

Monograph *a detailed written account of a single subject*

Abolitionist *a person who believed in the elimination of slavery*

Grand larceny *theft of a large sum of money or personal property*

Masthead *in publishing, the listing of pertinent information such as the editor, publisher, and writers*

Aphrodisiac *a substance rumored to cause increased sexual desire*

Expatriate *a person who lives outside his or her native country*

Temperance *to abstain from drinking alcohol*

Corpus delicti *a legal principle that asserts before a person can be convicted of a crime, there must be sufficient evidence that a crime was committed*

Pastoral *serene scenes depicting an idealized vision of life*

Monocle *a type of eyeglass worn on one eye, held in place by tensing the eye muscles*

Androgynous *displaying characteristics of both sexes*

Eccentric *to behave in an odd manner*

Barre *a horizontal bar used by ballerinas for support when practicing ballet positions*

Platonic *a non-sexual relationship*

Estranged *separated from*

Artistic signature *the distinct characteristics attributed to an artist, usually displayed in all of their work*

Improvisational *spontaneous or unplanned*

Protégée *a young female trained in their career by an experienced person*

Nomadic *traveling from place to place instead of having a fixed home*

Subsidiaries *smaller divisions of a larger company*

Jaunt *a trip*

Kibosh *to put an end to*

Bibliography

Introduction

Gajewski, Camille. "A Brief History of Women in Art (article)." *Khan Academy*. Tate, 2015. Web. 27 Dec. 2017.

Goldberg, Arlene. "Background on the Works Progress Administration (WPA)." *WomenArts*. WomenArts, 2009. Web. 02 Jan. 2018.

History.com Staff. "The Great Depression." *History.com*. A&E Television Networks, 2009. Web. 06 Jan. 2018.

Chapter 1

"Beauvoir." *Beauvoir*. Beauvoir, The Jefferson Davis Home and Presidential Library, n.d. Web. 04 Jan. 2018.

Crist, Linda Lasswell. "Beauvoir." *Mississippi History Now*. Mississippi Historical Society, June 2007. Web. 04 Jan. 2018.

Davis, Varina Anne. "A Romance of Summer Seas." *Google Books*. Originally Published by Harper & Brothers, 1899, 31 March 2011. Web. 19 Dec. 2017.

Davis, Varina Anne. "The Veiled Doctor." *Google Books*. Originally Published by Harper & Brothers, 1895, 22 May 2007. Web. 19 Dec. 2017.

Ferrell, Chiles Clifton. *The Daughter of the Confederacy Her Life, Character and Writings*. Mississippi Historical Society: 1899. *Internet Archives*. Internet Archives, 8 June 2009. Web. 4 Jan. 2018.

Find A Grave, database and images (https://www.findagrave.com: accessed 04 January 2018), memorial page for Alfred Wilkinson (9 Jun 1858–27 May 1918), Find A Grave Memorial no. 69810229, citing Oakwood Cemetery, Syracuse, Onondaga County, New York, USA; Maintained by Diane LM (contributor 47306054).

Lee, Heath Hardage. *Winnie Davis: Daughter of the Lost Cause*. Lincoln, NE: Potomac, an Imprint of the U of Nebraska, 2014. Print.

"Wordsmith." *Merriam-Webster.com*. Merriam-Webster, n.d. Web. 27 Dec. 2017.

Wyatt-Brown, Bertram. "Sarah Anne Ellis Dorsey: A Woman of Uncommon Mind." *Mississippi Historical Now*, Mississippi Historical Society, Mar. 2011.

Chapter 2

"Amelia Bloomer." *National Parks Service*. U.S. Department of the Interior, 26 Feb. 2015. Web. 4 Jan. 2018.

"Amelia Jenks Bloomer." *Humanrights.iowa.gov*. Iowa Department of Human Rights, n.d. Web. 6 Jan. 2018.

"The Amelia Bloomer Book List." *The American Library Association*. The American Library Association, n.d. Web. 07 Jan. 2018.

Angus, Kate. "List of Women-Run Presses." *VIDA: Women in Literary Arts*. VIDA, 31 Jan. 2016. Web. 09 Jan. 2018.

Holley, Joe. "Nancy Maynard, 61; Newspaper Owner Pressed for Diversity." *The Washington Post*. WP Company, 22 Sept. 2008. Web. 09 Jan. 2018.

"Meet Team Lily." *The Lily*. The Washington Post, 15 May 2017. Web. 04 Jan. 2018.

National Park Service. (n.d.). Amelia Bloomer – Publisher and advocate for Woman's Rights. *Social Welfare History Project*. Retrieved [04 January 2018]

Neal, Anthony. "Josephine St. Pierre Ruffin: A Pioneer in the Black Women's Club Movement." *Bay State Banner*. Bay State Banner, 3 Feb. 2006. Web. 06 Jan. 2018.

Chapter 3

Biography.com Editors. "Edmonia Lewis." *Biography.com*. A&E Networks Television, 01 Feb. 2017. Web. 02 Jan. 2018.

"Celebrating Edmonia Lewis." *Google*. Google, 1 Feb. 2017. Web. 20 Dec. 2017.

"Edmonia Lewis Center." *Oberlin College and Conservatory*. Oberlin College, n.d. Web. 20 Dec. 2017.

"Edmonia Lewis." *Smithsonian American Art Museum*. Smithsonian Institution, n.d. Web. 4 Jan. 2018.

Lavin, Talia. "The Life and Death of Edmonia Lewis, Spinster and Sculptor." *The Toast*. The Toast, 02 Nov. 2015. Web. 20 Dec. 2017.

Pickett, Mary. "Samuel W. Lewis: Orphan leaves mark on Bozeman" originally published in the Billings (Mont.) Gazette March 2, 2002 (Retrieved December 20, 2017).

Reno, Bobbi. "Edmonia Lewis Grave Restoration." *Gofundme.com*. Go-FundMe, 5 Apr. 2017. Web. 20 Dec. 2017.

"SEPIA SCULPTRESS: The Life and Trials of Edmonia Lewis 9/19/2015." *The Kennedy Center.* The John F. Kennedy Center for Performing Arts, n.d. Web. 9 Jan. 2018.

The Editors of Encyclopaedia Britannica. "Harriet Goodhue Hosmer." *Encyclopaedia Britannica*. Encyclopædia Britannica, Inc., 21 Feb. 2012. Web. 09 Jan. 2018.

"Visual Arts Fact Sheet."(n.d.): n. pag. *National Endowment for the Arts.* National Endowment for the Arts. Web. 9 Jan. 2018.

Willis-Abdurraqib, Hanif. "Olio by Tyehimba Jess." *The Rumpus.net.* The Rumpus, 06 Apr. 2016. Web. 9 Jan. 2018.

Chapter 4

"The Art of Romaine Brooks." *Smithsonian American Art Museum*, Smithsonian Institution, n.d. Web. 9 Jan. 2018.

Catlin, Roger. "The World Is Finally Ready to Understand Romaine Brooks."*Smithsonian.com*, Smithsonian Institution, 8 July 2016.

Frank, Priscilla. "Meet Romaine Brooks, A 20th Century Artist Who Paved The Way for The 21st Century Lesbian." *The Huffington Post*, TheHuffingtonPost.com, 19 May 2015.

Langer, Cassandra L. *Romaine Brooks: A Life*. Madison, WI: U of Wisconsin, 2015. Print.

Souhami, Diana. *Wild Girls: Paris, Sappho, and Art -- the Lives and Loves of Natalie Barney and Romaine Brooks*. New York: St. Martin's Griffin, 2007. Print.

Chapter Five

Adapted from the Essay by Robert Withers & Meira Goldberg. "Carmen Amaya." *Omayra Amaya Flamenco Dance Company*. Omayra Amaya Flamenco Dance Company, n.d. Web. 22 Jan. 2018.

"Carmen Amaya - Barcelona-born International Flamenco Star." *Barcelonas.com*. Barcelonas.com, n.d. Web. 20 Jan. 2018.

"Carmen Amaya." *IMDB*. IMDb.com, n.d. Web. 30 Jan. 2018.

Romain, Manuel. "La Legendaria Carmen Amaya, a 50 Años De Su Muerte." (The legendary Carmen Amaya, 50 years after her death) *Libertad Digital*. Libertad Digital, 21 Nov. 2013. Web. 22 Jan. 2018.

Sevilla, Paco. *Queen of the Gypsies: the Life and Legend of Carmen Amaya: Flamenco in the Theater Age, 1910-1960*. Sevilla Press, 1999.

The Editors of Encyclopaedia Britannica. "Spanish Civil War." *Encyclopaedia Britannica*, Encyclopaedia Britannica, Inc., 18 Sept. 2017.

Zatana, Estela. "Centennial Special: Carmen Amaya." *Deflamenco.com*. ADN Flamenco Web Services SL-Madrid, 13 May 2013. Web. 22 Jan. 2018.

Office, U.S. Copyright. "Performing Arts." *Copyright.gov*. Library of Congress, n.d. Web. 15 Mar. 2018.

Chapter Six

Biography.com Editors. "*Maria Tallchief.*" Biography.com. A&E Networks Television, 02 Apr. 2014. Web. 24 Jan. 2018.

Gourley, Catherine. *Who Is Maria Tallchief?* Grosset & Dunlap, 2002.

Halzack, Sarah. "Maria Tallchief, Ballet Star Who Was Inspiration for Balanchine, Dies at 88." *The Washington Post*. WP Company, 12 Apr. 2013. Web. 24 Jan. 2018.

Tallchief, Maria, and Larry Kaplan. *Maria Tallchief: America's Prima Ballerina*. New York: Henry Holt, 1997. Print.

Chapter 7

Hodges, Graham Russell. *Anna May Wong: From Laundryman's Daughter to Hollywood Legend*. New York: Palgrave Macmillan, 2004. Print.

Leibfried, Philip, and Chei Mi Lane. *Anna May Wong: A Complete Guide to Her Film, Stage, Radio, and Television Work*. Jefferson, NC: McFarland, 2004. Print.

User: Actingqueen13. "Asian Actors." *IMDb*. IMDb.com, Sept. 2017. Web. 21 Feb. 2018.

Chapter 8

Eckels, Carla, NO. "The Curious Case Of A Missing Academy Award." *National Public Radio, Inc.* National Public Radio, Inc., 22 Feb. 2009. Web. 9 Feb. 2018.

"Hattie McDaniel." *Los Angeles Times*. Los Angeles Times, n.d. Web. 21 Feb. 2018.

"Inductees." *Black Filmmakers Hall of Fame Archives*. Black Filmmakers Hall of Fame, n.d. Web. 2 Feb. 2018.

Petty, Miriam J. "Hattie McDaniel." *Stealing the Show: African American Performers and Audiences in 1930s Hollywood*. Oakland, CA: U of California, 2016. 27-71. Print.

Sangweni, Yolanda. "The Way-Too-Short List Of Black Oscar Winners." *Essence.com*. Essence Communications, 26 Feb. 2017. Web. 9 Feb. 2018.

U.S. Postal Service Historian. "African American Subjects on United States Postage Stamps." *USPS.com*. United States Postal Service, Feb. 2016. Web. 9 Feb. 2018.

Watts, Jill. *Hattie McDaniel: Black Ambition, White Hollywood*. New York: Amistad, 2005. Print.

Lynch, Hollis. "African American Life During the Depression and The New Deal" *Encyclopædia Britannica*. Encyclopædia Britannica, Inc., 28 Feb. 2018. Web. 13 Mar. 2018.

Snyder, Tom. "120 Years of American Education: A Statistical Portrait." *National Center for Education Statistics (NCES)*. U.S. Department of Education, 1993. Web. 14 Mar. 2018.

"Illiteracy Statistics and Demographics." *Statistic Brain*. Statistic Brain Research Institute, 20 Sept. 2017. Web. 14 Mar. 2018.

Nittle, Nadra Kareem. "5 Common Black Stereotypes in TV and Film." *ThoughtCo.* ThoughtCo., 13 Apr. 2017. Web. 14 Mar. 2018.

Chapter 9

"About Cathy Hughes." *CathyHughes.Com*. Cathy Hughes, 2016. Web. 13 Feb. 2018.

"Anna Mae Winburn." *Research Database of Archived Newspapers: Newspapers Library*. World Library Foundation, n.d. Web. 16 Feb. 2018.

Campbell, Alexia Fernandez, and Mauro Whiteman. "America's Largest Black Boarding School Sends 97 Percent of Students to College." *The Atlantic*. Atlantic Media Company, 12 Feb. 2015. Web. 16 Feb. 2018.

Deans, Karen. Swing Sisters: *The Story of the International Sweethearts of Rhythm*. New York: Holiday House, 2015. Print.

"Excellence in Education within a Christian Community." *The Piney Woods School*. The Piney Woods School, 2015. Web. 12 Feb. 2018.

Handy, Antoinette D. (1998-10-01). *The International Sweethearts of Rhythm: The Ladies' Jazz Band from Piney Woods Country Life School*. Scarecrow Press. 1–38, 207. Retrieved from Google Books, 14 Jan. 2018.

McDonough, John. "America's 'Sweethearts': An All-Girl Band That Broke Racial Boundaries." *NPR*. NPR, 22 Mar. 2011. Web. 12 Feb. 2018.

McDonough, John. "Honoring Jazz's Historic Sweethearts." *DownBeat.com*. Maher Publications, Apr. 2011. Web. 12 Feb. 2018.

"Music Makers: Helen Jones Woods." *The HistoryMakers*. The History-Makers, 6 Oct. 2007. Web. 16 Feb. 2018.

Nelson, Marilyn. *Sweethearts of Rhythm: The Story of the Greatest All-girl Swing Band in the World*. New York: Dial, 2009. Print.

"Pauline Braddy Williams, Swing-Era Singer, Dies At 73." *The Washington Post*. WP Company, 02 Feb. 1996. Web. 17 Feb. 2018.

"Pauline Braddy: Biography & History." *AllMusic*. AllMusic, n.d. Web. 17 Feb. 2018.

"Press Kit." *Diva Jazz Orchestra*. Diva Jazz Orchestra, n.d. Web. 11 Feb. 2018.

Schiller, G. (Director). (1986). International Sweethearts of Rhythm [Video file]. Jezebel Productions. Retrieved February 16, 2018, from Kanopy.

Schiller, G. (Director). (1996). Tiny and Ruby: Hell Divin' Women [Video file]. Jezebel Productions. Retrieved February 16, 2018, from Kanopy.

Smithsonian Videos. "Women and Jazz: International Sweethearts of Rhythm." *YouTube.com* YouTube, 10 Apr. 2011. Web. 9 Feb. 2018.

"The Piney Woods School." *National Center for Educational Statistics.* U.S. Department of Education, n.d. Web. 14 Mar. 2018.

Chapter 10

Das, Kavita. "Lakshmi Shankar Shares Her Memories of Uday Shankar, Recalls His Legendary Film 'Kalpana'." *The Aerogram.* Ladoos, LLC, 23 May 2013. Web. 7 Feb. 2018.

"Hindustani Classical Music." *New World Encyclopedia.* New World Encyclopedia, 24 Dec. 2017. Web. 17 Feb. 2018.

Hunt, Ken. "Lakshmi Shankar: Vocalist Who Worked with Her Brother-in-law Ravi and Sang on the Soundtrack to Attenborough's 'Gandhi'." *The Independent.* Independent Digital News and Media, 02 Apr. 2014. Web. 13 Feb. 2018.

"Interview with Smt. Lakshmi Shankar." *Kathaka.* Chitresh Das Dance Company & Chhandam School of Kathak, 23 Nov. 2010. Web. 12 Feb. 2018.

Isal, Shireen. "Interview with Lakshmi Shankar." *Association Sargam.* Association Sargam, June 2001. Web. 14 Feb. 2018.

Kannikeswaran, Kannis. "Goodbye, Lakshmi Shankar." *The Hindu.* The Hindu, 07 Jan. 2014. Web. 14 Feb. 2018.

Khan, Faizal. "Unsung Heroines." *The Caravan.* The Caravan, 17 Nov. 2016. Web. 9 Feb. 2018.

"Lakshmi Shankar." *Alliance for California Traditional Arts.* Alliance for California Traditional Arts, 2012. Web. 14 Feb. 2018.

"Pleurisy." *WebMD.* WebMD, n.d. Web. 17 Feb. 2018.

Ramnarayan, Gowri. "Making Music, With Love." *The Hindu.* The Hindu, 1 Jan. 2001. Web. 13 Feb. 2018.

The Editors of Encyclopaedia Britannica. "Ravi Shankar." *Encyclopædia Britannica.* Encyclopædia Britannica, Inc., 12 Jan. 2018. Web. 17 Feb. 2018.

Tsering, Lisa. "Classical Vocalist Lakshmi Shankar Passes Away." *Wayback Machine.* Indiawest.com, 2 Jan. 2014. Web. 14 Feb. 2018.

Myra Faye Turner is a writer, poet, avid coffee drinker, and children's books author. She has written several books for Atlantic Publishing including *The Young Adult's Guide to Identity Theft: A Step-by-Step Guide to Stopping Scammers* and *So You Want to Publish Your Own Book & E-Book: A Step-by-Step Guide to Fun & Profitable Publishing.* She lives in New Orleans, Louisiana with her teenage son, Tyler.

Index